Château Thierry & Belleau Wood 1918

America's baptism of fire on the Marne

Campaign • 177

Château Thierry & Belleau Wood 1918

America's baptism of fire on the Marne

David Bonk • Illustrated by Peter Dennis

First published in Great Britain in 2007 by Osprey Publishing,
Midland House, West Way, Botley, Oxford OX2 0PH, UK
443 Park Avenue South, New York, NY 10016, USA
E-mail: info@ospreypublishing.com

A CIP catalog record for this book is available from the British Library

ISBN: 978 1 84603 034 5

Page layout by: The Black Spot
Index by Alison Worthington
Typeset in Helvetica Neue and ITC New Baskerville
Maps by The Map Studio
3D bird's-eye views by The Black Spot
Originated by United Graphic, Singapore
Printed in China through Worldprint

07 08 09 10 11   10 9 8 7 6 5 4 3 2 1

For a catalog of all books published by Osprey Military and Aviation please
contact:

NORTH AMERICA
Osprey Direct, c/o Random House Distribution Center, 400 Hahn Road,
Westminster, MD 21157
E-mail: info@ospreydirect.com

ALL OTHER REGIONS
Osprey Direct UK, P.O. Box 140 Wellingborough, Northants, NN8 2FA, UK
E-mail: info@ospreydirect.co.uk

www.ospreypublishing.com

Dedication

To my wife, Jackie, without whose support and
encouragement I would not have been able to complete
this project.

Acknowledgments

My hope is that this book will provide new insights into this
pivotal battle. America's involvement in and contributions
to World War I have been largely overshadowed by the
American experience in World War II. I want to thank the
staff at the United States National Archives and the Robert
McCormick Research Center at the Cantigny First Division
Foundation for their help with the book.

Artist's note

Readers may care to note that the original paintings from
which the color plates in this book were prepared are
available for private sale. All reproduction copyright
whatsoever is retained by the Publishers. All inquiries
should be addressed to:

Peter Dennis
Fieldhead
The Park
Mansfield
Nottinghamshire
NG18 2AT

The Publishers regret that they can enter into no
correspondence upon this matter.

Editor's note

Unless otherwise stated all images are in the public
domain.

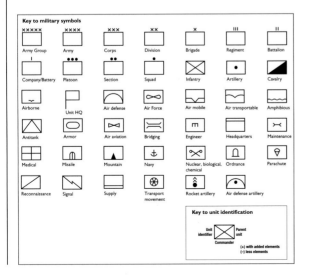

CONTENTS

ORIGINS OF THE CAMPAIGN   7

CHRONOLOGY   11

OPPOSING COMMANDERS   12
American Commanders • German Commanders

OPPOSING ARMIES   15
The Americans • The Germans • The French • Orders of Battle

OPPOSING PLANS   22
German Plans • American Plans

AMERICA ENTERS THE WAR   24
First Blood • Cantigny • Operation *Blücher*

CHÂTEAU-THIERRY AND BELLEAU WOOD   41
Château-Thierry • Belleau Wood • Hill 142 • Attack on Belleau Wood • Vaux

AFTERMATH   91

THE BATTLEFIELD TODAY   93

BIBLIOGRAPHY   94

INDEX   95

Marine snipers like these were used to harass Germans in the northern section of Belleau Wood.

American artillery supporting the Marine attacks in Belleau Wood. The Americans were slow to realize the value of appropriate artillery preparation prior to launching their assaults.

ORIGINS OF THE CAMPAIGN

I n early 1918, World War I had reached a crisis point for the British and French. The stalemate of the previous four years was about to be broken by a combination of factors. The failed offensives of 1917 had left the British Army exhausted and the French Army on the verge of widespread mutiny.

By late 1917, the Allies had concluded that the state of the British and French armies prohibited any significant offensive initiatives in 1918. The French Commander-in-Chief, Henri Pétain, in an effort to quell the continuing mutinies, promised that the French Army would not engage in offensive actions until the Americans arrived. Allied commanders agreed that they would act largely on the defensive, waiting for the consolidation and training of the American forces to be completed before going back on the offensive to defeat the Germans in 1919. The entry of America into the war in April 1917 had bolstered Allied hopes, although the organization of an American army in France had been slow.

Unfortunately, the Germans also recognized that the intervention of American manpower and manufacturing would be decisive in the outcome of the war. German propaganda began a campaign to belittle the fighting capabilities of the American Army. Newspapers characterized the Americans as degenerates and reluctant conscripts, who wept as they were herded aboard the transports. One newspaper wrote, "Our soldiers despise them and do not consider them worthy enemies."

German storm troopers rush through the wire. The soldier at the far left holds a hand grenade. Note the wire cutters carried by the soldier on the far right.

With the collapse of Imperial Russia in early 1918, the German High Command saw an opportunity to strike a decisive blow on the Western Front before the growing strength of the Americans could shift the strategic balance towards the Allies. German Gen Ludendorff and his staff began planning Operation *Michael*, designed to shatter the brittle British/French front. The centerpiece of the German offensive would be the deployment of specially trained "*stoss*" or storm trooper attack units. These units emphasized close coordination with artillery and rapid movement, bypassing enemy strongpoints and striking deep into the enemy rear to spread confusion. Nearly one quarter of the German infantry divisions preparing to storm the Allied positions were designated "attack divisions," provided with the newest equipment, including light machine guns.

In early 1918, the British and French began to implement a more sophisticated defensive arrangement, made up of forward, battle, and rear zones, each featuring successive lines of trenches, mutually supporting strongpoints, and machine-gun emplacements constructed to provide all-round defense. The British Fifth Army, the main target of Operation *Michael*, had only recently been required to extend its lines to Barisis, further extending its front. In addition, not all British officers completely understood the new defensive arrangements and the Fifth Army's forward zone was too densely occupied.

Operation *Michael* struck the British on March 21, 1918, destroying the British Fifth Army and penetrating almost 40 miles. For two weeks the Germans battered the Allies, but failed to achieve their ultimate objective of capturing Amiens and splitting the French and British armies. By April 5, the German offensive sputtered to a halt and both sides sought to catch their breath before the next blow fell. During the *Michael* offensive the British armies slowly edged towards the Channel coast, while the French shifted their armies south towards Paris. As the Allied armies staggered under the German attacks a consensus was reached among the increasingly acrimonious Allied leaders to appoint

French forces, with two Hotchkiss machine guns, defend a strongpoint against the German spring offensive.

French forces, with two Hotchkiss machine guns, defend a strongpoint against the German spring offensive.

French Gen Foch to act temporarily as supreme commander, to ensure a coordinated response to future attacks. Foch's role as supreme commander was made permanent on April 14.

The German offensive distracted the British and French leaders from their ongoing struggle with American Commander-in-Chief John J. Pershing over the deployment of the American Army. Since the first American units landed in France, Pershing had resisted strong Allied pressure to integrate American soldiers into existing British and French armies. With Pershing's rejection of proposed amalgamation and the establishment of separate training camps for American troops, the British and French openly questioned the fighting effectiveness of the American Army.

The dispute between Pershing and the Allies was due to a fundamental difference in philosophy. Pershing, for his part, believed the war would not be won by fighting between trenches in no man's land. He believed that only breakthrough and open maneuver would allow one side or the other to win a decisive victory, and he directed that American troops be trained accordingly. The success of the German offensive seemed to confirm his position, as the British and French reeled back along a broad front. At the same time as American divisions in training occupied front-line trenches, divisional headquarters staff collected as many reports as they could concerning the nature of the fighting in the north. These reports noted the absence of large-scale defensive works and the emphasis placed on tactical mobility.

As the German offensive pushed back the French and British it also produced 350,000 casualties, creating a manpower crisis. British Prime Minister Lloyd George used the fresh crisis to renew the British call for the amalgamation of American infantry and machine-gun units into existing British units. Pershing held firm, suggesting that the Allies amalgamate their weakened divisions and allow American divisions to enter the line as they became available. In recognition of the crisis Pershing did agree to a temporary modification to the shipping schedule, allowing the British to transport only infantry and machine-gun units, as long as the divisional signal, engineer, and headquarters staff accompanied the units. Despite his continued misgivings about Allied proposals for deploying the American Army, Pershing responded to the growing crisis by offering American forces to Foch.

On April 9, 1918, the Germans launched a smaller offensive, codenamed *Georgette*, directed at a weak sector held by Portuguese divisions north of the La Bassee Canal. The German attack shattered the Portuguese, pushing the front back over 3 miles. On April 10, the second phase of *Georgette* opened with the German Fourth Army driving towards Havrincourt, capturing Messines and part of the Messines–Wytschaete Ridge. This new crisis, which threatened to drive a wedge between the British and French armies, caused Gen Douglas Haig, British Supreme Commander, to issue his now-famous "backs to the wall" address. On April 11, Haig released his Order of the Day, which stated, "Every position must be held to the last man: there must be no retreat. With our backs to the wall and believing in the justice of our cause, each one of us must fight to the end."

As the British reinforced their positions against the new break-through, Ludendorff shifted his pressure once more. Attempting to strike again towards Amiens on April 24, the Germans captured Villers-Bretonneux. Although the British launched a timely counterattack on April 25, recapturing Villers-Bretonneux, the German Alpine Corps inflicted a serious setback against them, capturing Mount Kemmel. Despite these successes the German offensive began to lose steam and finally was called off on April 29, leaving both sides to regroup and consider their next move.

While Ludendorff's ultimate goal was to shatter the British in Flanders, as *Georgette* ground to a halt he decided to attack the French in order to draw their reserves away from the British. The result was planning for Operation *Blücher*, focused on attacking the French along the Chemin des Dames on the Aisne River.

The nature of Belleau Wood provided strong defensive positions and allowed the Germans to infiltrate American positions throughout the battle.

CHRONOLOGY

1917

January 19	German Foreign Minister Zimmerman proposes that Mexico provide assistance to Germany in the event of war with the United States. In return, Zimmerman promises Mexico American territory.
April 6	US Congress declares war on Germany.
June 13	Gen John Pershing and staff leave London for France.
June 26	American 1st Division and 5th Marine Regiment land in France.
September–October	Remainder of American 2nd Division lands in France.
September–December	American 26th and 42nd Divisions land in France.
December 15	Armistice of Brest-Litovsk ends fighting on the Eastern Front.

1918

January 21	Ludendorff decides on Operation *Michael*, sets offensive to start March 15.
March 1–12	Germany deploys army for Operation *Michael*. Offensive delayed to March 21.
March 16–19	Germans move 60 divisions into position for start of offensive.
March 21	Ludendorff begins Operation *Michael*.
April 9	Operation *Georgette* begins in Flanders.
April 20	German attack on 26th Division at Seicheprey.
April 24	American 1st Division deployed in Montdidier sector.
May 27	Operation *Blücher* drives French from Chemin des Dames.
May 28	1st Division attacks and captures village of Cantigny.
May 31	Elements of American 3rd Division ordered to Château-Thierry.
June 1	2nd Division ordered to defend Paris–Metz road. Germans occupy Belleau Wood and village of Bouresches.
June 3	German drive to Paris is stopped by 5th Marines at Les Mares Farm.
June 4	3rd Division completes move to Château-Thierry.
June 6	5th and 6th Marines capture Hill 142, village of Bouresches, and occupy southern portion of Belleau Wood. Bloodiest day in Marine Corps' history.
June 8	Germans and Marines trade attacks in Belleau Wood.
June 9–13	Ludendorff opens Operation *Gneisenau*. German Army advances 10 miles before being stopped before Compiègne.
June 10	Marines advance into center of Belleau Wood.
June 12	Marines advance into northern portion of Belleau Wood.
June 15	7th Infantry Regiment relieves Marines in Belleau Wood.
June 16–22	7th Regiment fails to drive Germans from Belleau Wood.
June 22	Marines relieve 7th Regiment.
June 23	Marine attack on northern portion of Belleau Wood fails.
June 25	Marines capture Belleau Wood.
July 1	9th Regiment captures village of Vaux.
July 4	Soldiers from American 2nd Division march in Paris parade commemorating American Independence Day. Elements of American 131st and 132nd regiments, 33rd Division, support Australian 4th Division in attack at Hamel.
July 15–17	German Operation *Rheims* achieves minimal gains. American 3rd, 26th, 28th, and 42nd Divisions participate in stopping German offensive.
July 18–August 6	French/American Aisne-Marne offensive. French XX Corps spearheads attack. American 1st and 2nd Divisions and French Moroccan Division lead main assault near Soissons.
August 8–November 11	British begin Somme offensive. Initial attack includes American 33rd and 80th Divisions as part of British Fourth Army.
August 18–November 11	French Oise-Aisne offensive. American 32nd Division captures Juvigny, August 30, 1918. American III Corps part of French Sixth Army.
August 19–November 11	British Ypres-Lys offensive. British Second and Fifth Armies, including American II Corps, eliminate Lys salient. Pershing responds to Foch's request for reinforcements by sending 37th and 91st Divisions in mid-October, 1918.
September 12–16	American St Mihiel offensive. Pershing's first major offensive aimed at reducing the St Mihiel salient. 650,000 men, including 550,000 Americans and 100,000 Allied troops, take part in attack.
September 26–November 11	Meuse-Argonne offensive. Combined Allied offensive includes 1.2 million American troops.
October 24–November 4	Amercian 332nd Regiment participates in Italian attack against Austrians at battle of Vittorio Veneto.

OPPOSING COMMANDERS

AMERICAN COMMANDERS

John Joseph Pershing taught school for several years before entering West Point in 1882 at the age of 22. After graduating in 1886, Pershing served with the 6th Cavalry on the western frontier. He taught military science at the University of Nebraska and at the same time earned a law degree. Pershing served in the Spanish-American War followed by three tours in the Philippines battling the Moro insurgency. He went to Japan as military attaché and studied the evolution of warfare during the 1905 Russo-Japanese conflict.

President Theodore Roosevelt promoted Pershing, who had married the daughter of a Republican senator, to brigadier general over the heads of 862 other officers in 1906. Pershing then served as Governor of Moro province in the Philippines before being selected in 1915 to command the American forces pursuing Pancho Villa in Mexico. Pershing's command in the southwest provided him with experience overseeing an American expeditionary force dependent on long supply lines. More importantly, Pershing's performance impressed President Woodrow Wilson and his Secretary of War, Newton Baker. In particular, the President and Secretary credited Pershing for his strict adherence to their initial instructions intended to limit American intervention in Mexico.

Pershing was appointed to command the American Army in Europe in May, 1917. In May 1918, Pershing offered Marshal Foch the immediate

Brigadier General James Harbord, US Army (seated), commanded the 4th Brigade in the 2nd Division. Harbord would play a central role in the coming struggle for Belleau Wood. Harbord's staff, (standing) included a mix of Marines and US Army. The three officers directly behind Harbord are Marines, distinguished by the anchor and globe insignia on their collars and the pleated breast pockets of their coats.

Commander of American Armies, General John J. Pershing with Marshal Foch in April, 1918. Despite continuing disagreements with the French and British over the deployment of American units, Pershing offered Foch the use of American troops.

deployment of American troops to stem the German advance which had shattered the French defenses along the Chemin des Dames. Elements of the 3rd Division stopped the German advance at Château-Thierry, while the 2nd Division stopped the Germans on the road to Paris.

James Harbord enlisted in the Army in 1889 and served with the 10th US Cavalry, where he became acquainted with Capt John Pershing. In 1902, he was promoted to the position of Chief of the Philippine Constabulary. When the US entered the war in 1917, Harbord was chosen by Pershing as the American Expeditionary Force's chief of staff in France. In May, 1918, Harbord was reassigned by Pershing to the Marine Brigade of the 2nd Infantry Division. Harbord's appointment to command a brigade of Marines caused some controversy. Harbord was responsible for coordinating the disposition of the 4th Brigade with the French to stop the German advance. Harbord directed the battle to recapture Belleau Wood, but his tactics were uninspired, and his reluctance to employ adequate artillery preparation contributed to the heavy casualties among the Marines throughout the battle.

Albertus Catlin was a graduate of the United States Naval Academy and commanded the 40-man Marine detachment aboard the USS *Maine*. Catlin survived the explosion that destroyed the *Maine* in Havana, and fought with additional Marine units during the Spanish-American War. Promoted to major, Catlin commanded the Marines assigned to the fleet which landed at Vera Cruz, Mexico, in 1914, where he earned the Congressional Medal of Honor. He was given command of the 6th Marine Regiment, which together with the 5th Marine Regiment formed the 4th Brigade. Catlin was given command of the Marine assault on June 6, 1918. His deployment and instructions for the attack, coupled with Harbord's unwillingness to utilize adequate artillery, resulted in mass casualties among the Marines. Catlin was wounded early on June 6, and played no part in the subsequent struggle to capture Belleau Wood.

Logan Feland commanded a company of Kentucky infantry during the Spanish-American War, and was appointed first lieutenant in the Marine Corps in 1899. Feland served throughout Central America for the next decade and participated in the Vera Cruz invasion in 1914. Promoted to lieutenant colonel in 1917, Feland served as executive officer for the 5th Regiment. With the wounding of Col Catlin on June 6, 1918, and the subsequent breakdown of command during the confused fighting inside Belleau Wood, Feland was given command of elements of both the 5th and 6th Marines. Feland provided important leadership during the remainder of the battle and won the Distinguished Service Cross.

Frederic Wise was commissioned in 1899 in the United States Marine Corps and retired in 1926 after 27 years, with the rank of brigadier general. Wise was a veteran of the Philippine Insurrection, Boxer Rebellion, and American intervention at Vera Cruz, Mexico. Wise played a critical role at Belleau Wood, leading the 2/5th Marines in the June 10 attack that resulted in the capture of the lower portion of the wood. Wise's failure to accurately determine his location in Belleau Wood and his premature claims of capturing the wood brought him into conflict with Brig Gen Harbord. Although relieved of command by Harbord on June 18, 1918, Wise was awarded the US Navy Distinguished Service Medal for his actions at Belleau Wood. Wise would later command the 59th Infantry Regiment in the St Mihiel and the Meuse-Argonne campaigns.

GERMAN COMMANDERS

Eric Ludendorff was the mastermind of the German offensives of early 1918. Between 1904 and 1913, Ludendorff served as a staff officer and was appointed chief of staff in East Prussia at the outbreak of the war. In combination with von Hindenburg, Ludendorff won decisive victories at Tannenberg (1914) and Masurian Lakes (1915). In 1916, Ludendorff was appointed quartermaster general. In partnership with Hindenburg, Ludendorff pressured Kaiser Wilhelm to dismiss officers who supported a negotiated peace settlement. In July, 1917, Ludendorff took effective control over all aspects of the German war effort. With the withdrawal of Russia from the war, Ludendorff conceived the offensives intended to win the war in the West before the Americans could tip the balance. Ludendorff initiated Operation *Blücher* on May 27, 1918. Originally intended to draw French reserves south in preparation for resumption of the main offensive against the British, the success of the attack induced Ludendorff to push on with the goal of threatening Paris.

Georg Bruchmuller entered the German artillery in 1885. He was retired as a lieutenant colonel in 1913 for medical reasons but recalled in late 1914 as the war expanded, and was assigned to the 86th Division on the Eastern Front. Bruchmuller began developing innovative artillery tactics that emphasized intense barrages of relatively short duration, designed to disrupt rather than destroy enemy formations. Bruchmuller's tactics also included shifting targets frequently and concentrating fire at command centers and other strategic points behind the front lines. Bruchmuller demonstrated the effectiveness of his tactics in 1916 at Lake Naroch, and at Riga in 1917. Bruchmuller was transferred to the West and coordinated artillery support for Ludendorff's spring offensives. He organized the opening artillery barrage for Operation *Georgette* that devastated the French defenders and allowed the German infantry to drive towards Paris.

Oskar von Hutier commanded a division in the opening campaigns against Belgium and France in 1914. Transferred to the Eastern Front in 1915 and given command of a corps in the Tenth Army, von Hutier spent the next several years developing innovative infantry tactics that were designed to break the stalemate of trench warfare. In September 1917, von Hutier, commanding the German Eighth Army, captured Riga using the new tactics, which were soon adopted by the Germans in other theaters. German troops successfully routed the Italians at Caporetto using von Hutier's tactics, and Ludendorff transferred von Hutier to the West in early 1918 to train his assault divisions for the coming spring offensives. Von Hutier's tactical innovations, combined with similar artillery tactics developed by Bruchmuller, allowed the German Army to break open the Western Front and created the most serious crisis of the war for the Allies.

OPPOSING ARMIES

THE AMERICANS

I n May 1917, Gen John J. Pershing was appointed commander-in-chief of the American Expeditionary Force. Pershing developed strategic and tactical doctrine based largely on his observations of the conduct of the war to that point. Prior to America's entry into the war, American general staff monitored battlefield developments and assessed the strengths and shortcomings of both Allied and German strategic initiatives. Many of these activities drew criticism from officials in the Wilson administration, who were sensitive to even the appearance that the United States had any interest in the events unfolding in Europe. A policy of strict neutrality limited the development of a more extensive program of intelligence gathering.

Once war was declared, a small cadre of American officers joined British and French units at the front and sought to glean additional lessons from their ongoing experiences. In July 1917, Pershing increased the size of the infantry company from 150 to 250, reflecting the need to create a tactical unit that would adequately integrate the different types of weapons systems necessary to survive on the battlefield. Pershing's directive also reflected the lessons of battlefield attrition. The increased size of the company was designed to ensure that the unit could absorb high casualty rates and still function on the battlefield. Another decision that would have long-term implications for the American involvement was to organize American divisions with two brigades of two regiments each, totaling almost 28,000 men, twice the size of standard British, French, or German divisions.

American soldier engaged in bayonet practice. Although proficiency with the bayonet was not part of Pershing's vision of open warfare, this skill would prove to be invaluable in the coming hand-to-hand combat in the confused fighting for villages and clearing of woods.

These Marines undergo practice throwing hand grenades under the eyes of their French instructors. Although discouraged by the French, in combat the Americans abandoned the stiff throwing motion in favor of the more familiar motion of throwing a baseball.

During this period, Pershing also enumerated a controversial tactical training doctrine. He was committed to reinforcing the traditional American emphasis on targeted rifle fire and open maneuver. By 1917, both the French and British had largely adopted a defensive tactical doctrine, the result of their experience in the trenches. American staff dismissed the French and British focus on static warfare. Pershing envisioned the American Army taking the offensive, and directed that American units be trained in appropriate tactics. He initially resisted the offer of British and French assistance to set up and train the American armies in favor of American-based training programs. However, the sheer scale of the demands to train and equip the rapidly growing American Army gave mixed results. French and British trainers would, after all, be needed and, as feared, they focused their training on a continuation of trench warfare.

Marine Lt Col Frederic Wise described the training his 5th Marine battalion received from the French 115th Chasseurs Alpins in early 1918:

We dug a series of trenches. We took up the new method of bayonet fighting. Long lines of straw-stuffed figures hanging from a crossbeam between two upright posts were set up. The men fixed bayonets and charged them. British instructors, who had arrived shortly after us, stood over them and urged them on… The British at this time were crazy about the bayonet. They knew it was going to win the war. The French were equally obsessed with the grenade. They knew it was going to win the war. So we also got a full dose of training in hand grenade throwing.

Special schools were set up to provide in-depth training of American officers, where French instructors provided classes on tactics for employing 37mm guns, machine guns, automatic rifles, and grenades. American policy still embraced open warfare and firepower without defining exactly how and under what conditions these tactics were to be employed, so this training left commanders with a confused sense of just how they were to deploy their men and which tactics to use. This confusion would become evident as the Americans took up positions and entered into battle. The response of American officers and their men was to develop tactics that integrated elements of what they had learned and evolved in response to the reality of the battlefield.

The composition of the American Army that was being organized for combat in Europe reflected the composition of contemporary American society. In 1917, nearly one third of the American population was either foreign-born or the children of foreign-born parents. Nearly 20 percent of the American Army was foreign-born, primarily from southern or eastern Europe. The challenges of integrating recruits with little or no command of the English language were further complicated by the infusion of large numbers of rural youth, nearly 25 percent of whom were illiterate. While the officers training the Army noted that these farmboys eventually made the best soldiers, they tended to have the least formal education and required longer training periods. The rapid expansion of the American Army strained efforts to provide adequate training and to produce non-commissioned officers and officers in adequate numbers.

In addition to the organization of units through the amalgamation of regular Army and National Guard units, buttressed by conscripts, the American Army witnessed a dramatic expansion of the United States Marine Corps. During the war, the Marines grew from approximately 500 officers and 13,000 men to over 65,000 men. The declaration of war was met initially with an outpouring of volunteers for all branches of the armed services and the Marines were no exception. Many of the earliest officer recruits were from leading American colleges and universities, further adding to the popular image of the Marines as an elite force.

The Marines were able to establish a cadre of experienced soldiers, particularly non-commissioned officers, around which they organized their infantry regiments and machine-gun battalions. Standards for enlistment were higher in the Corps than other branches, and it is estimated that 80 percent of volunteers were rejected. The Corps training program emphasized marksmanship and physical endurance. Over 67 percent of the Marines arriving in France in 1917 were qualified as a marksman, sharpshooter, or expert rifleman. These skills would prove invaluable in the defensive struggle to stop the German advance.

The American Army was organized around a 250-man company, made up of four platoons of 59 men and a small headquarters group.

This recruiting poster from 1918 recognized the polyglot composition of the American Army, integrating the immigrants of many nations. The training of the Army was complicated by lack of education and proficiency in the English language.

"Company of Nations" was the title of this promotional photo, designed to illustrate the diverse nature of the American Army. A close examination of the faces reveals the variety of nationalities and races.

Marine recruiting posters focused on the fighting spirit of the Marine Corps. Later posters highlighted the Marine's role in the opening battles of America's involvement, boasting that the Marines were "First to Fight."

Each platoon was composed of a headquarters unit and four squads, which varied in size from 9 to 15 men. The organization of the platoon mirrored the tactical emphasis on fire and maneuver. The first squad of 12 men was designated as grenadiers. The second squad of nine men was issued modified versions of the French VB *tromblon* rifle grenade discharger. The third squad, composed of 17 riflemen, was expected, in conjunction with the first squad, to be the main maneuver element of the platoon. The fourth squad, which included 15 men with four Chauchat automatic rifles, was expected to provide fire support, along with the rifle grenadiers of the second squad. Four companies organized around a small battalion headquarters composed a battalion.

In turn, three battalions made up each regiment. The regiment was further supplemented by a 350-man headquarters element, which included three 37mm support guns and six 3in mortars. Also included at the regimental level was a heavy machine-gun company composed of 16 guns and 178 men. During the course of the coming battles the heavy machine guns were deployed in a variety of roles. During the initial attacks on June 6, 1918, the guns were grouped together and used to fire a preparatory barrage intended to suppress the Germans. The guns were later deployed in smaller sections to support localized defenses.

American infantry companies were also supplemented by the deployment of engineering companies, who assisted in the construction of defensive positions, and were routinely called upon to act as infantry as American losses increased. During the course of the struggle for Belleau Wood the depleted Marine companies were strengthened by the infusion of replacements from composite training battalions. Most of these men had only recently completed basic training in the United States. Their inexperience would result in many casualties. Marine replacements could easily be identified by the traditional forest-green Marine uniforms they wore, in comparison to the veterans who had replaced their worn-out clothes from Army stocks.

The American brigade organization included two infantry regiments, supplemented by support units including a machine-gun battalion of 64 guns. In turn, an American infantry division, totaling over 28,000 men, included two brigades. Field artillery units were assigned at the divisional level, and usually composed of two 75mm regiments and one 155mm regiment, each with 24 guns. One 6in trench mortar battery, 12 guns, was also assigned to the divisional organization.

While the theoretical army organization suggested that divisions could rely on additional support from units assigned at the corps or army level, the American Army had yet to be completely organized, and American units thrown into battle in May 1918 were assigned to existing French corps. Although the French did provide some supplemental artillery support, for the most part the American divisions were required to act independently during the course of the coming battle. Despite the directive from Pershing to emphasize open maneuver warfare, the practical result of having to rely on French trainers resulted in the Americans favoring the "line of sections" formation when attacking. This standard French formation required that each company formed a two-platoon front, with two platoons following. Each platoon was divided into four sections, with two forward and two behind.

The basic infantry weapon of the American Army in early 1918 was the 1903 Model Springfield. The Springfield was very accurate, firing a .30 caliber bullet from a five-round clip. The rifle was somewhat shorter and lighter than the standard German *Gewehr* 98, making it more effective in the confined spaces of the trenches. The Springfield was coupled with the 18in M1905 bayonet. Although the Springfield was the preferred infantry weapon, America began the war with limited quantities. While the Marine Brigade used the Springfield exclusively, the regular army regiments in 1st and 2nd divisions included a mix of Springfield and P14 Enfields. Officers, senior NCOs, and specialty troops were issued the 1911 Colt handgun. US forces also utilized Winchester shotguns, which proved effective in the close quarters of Belleau Wood. Although poorly designed and unreliable, the French Chauchat light machine gun was issued to all the 1st and 2nd divisions. For heavy machine guns the Americans had been issued the Hotchkiss.

While the 1st Division had a core of veterans in its ranks, it also included large numbers of new soldiers. The 2nd Division's composition was similar, although the Marine Brigade boasted a nucleus of veterans. The longer training period and time spent in the trenches afforded both divisions an opportunity to gain valuable experience under fire. As newspaperman Floyd remarked, "Our army knew nothing but confidence."

THE GERMANS

The German Army facing the Americans was a mix of veteran units supplemented by reserve units. In preparation for the March offensive, the German troops received several weeks of comprehensive tactical training, in most cases under the direction of veteran storm troopers. The training focused on small unit leadership, rifle marksmanship, and implementation of the new weapons. Although the Germans had been able to reinforce their Western Front armies with veteran units from the East following the collapse of the Russian Army, the successes of March and April had resulted in crippling numbers of casualties, reducing the effectiveness of front-line units. German infantry organization in 1918 included three battalions to each regiment, three regiments to each brigade, and two brigades formed a division. The effective strength of most companies was about 150 men. Each infantry battalion had four companies, each company comprised three platoons. The establishment strength of each German rifle company was approximately 260 men. The platoons, ranging in size from 36 to 45 men, included two light machine guns.

Standard German defensive tactical doctrine called for the deployment of one battalion at the front, supported by a second battalion approximately one kilometer behind. The support battalion was expected to reinforce the front-line battalion. The third battalion was placed in reserve usually beyond hostile artillery range. The reserve battalion was assigned the role of counterattacking to regain lost ground, or providing an additional line of defense in the event of a breakthrough.

The standard German infantry rifle was the *Gewehr* 98, capable of firing five rounds from an internal magazine. While the rifle was suitable for open warfare it proved less useful in the trenches. The *Karabiner* 98 was the standard carbine adopted by storm trooper units. It was somewhat shorter than the *Gewehr* but no less effective. In late spring, 1918, the MP18 sub-machine gun began to be issued to German units. The standard German sidearm was the *Pistole* '08, or Luger handgun. German regular infantry and storm trooper units used both the M1915 *Stielhandgranate*, stick handle grenade, and the *Eierhandgranate* or "egg grenade." The standard German heavy machine gun was the *Maschinen-Gewehr* '08 Maxim machine gun. The Maxim was supplemented by the Model '08/15 light machine gun. Weighing 19.5kg (43lb), it provided increased mobility over the Maxim, which weighed 63.3kg (140lb). Each infantry battalion had available six 76mm *minenwerfers* mortars and a Maxim heavy machine-gun company, and each infantry company included six Model '08/15 light machine guns. Artillery support at divisional level included three 77mm batteries and three 105mm howitzer batteries; each had a battery of four guns.

The Germans facing the 1st Division at Cantigny were part of the 82nd Reserve Division, XXVI Corps. The German IV Reserve Corps, known as Corps Conta after its commander, included nine divisions. Corps Conta, a mix of verteran and conscript units, was assigned the task of breeching the Marne River at Château-Thierry and capturing the Paris–Metz road. The 10th Division was rated as a first class combat unit, while the 28th and 36th were second class, and the 237th and 87th were fourth class.

The German 1918 spring offensive, beginning with Operation *Michael* in March, included the widespread use of "infiltration" tactics, conceived by Oskar von Hutier. This doctrine emphasized short artillery bombardments, followed by creeping barrages that allowed German shock troops, storm troopers, to penetrate enemy defenses at weak points. The primary objective was to capture or destroy headquarter and artillery units deployed behind the main line of defense. While the storm troopers bypassed enemy strongpoints, German infantry, supported by heavy machine guns and mortars, were expected to overwhelm the enemy defensive line, now punctured, disoriented, and unable to rely on direction from headquarters or effective artillery support. Finally, reserve units would mop up remaining pockets of resistance.

At Château-Thierry and Les Mares Farm the Germans, believing they were pursuing dispirited and disorganized French units, failed to organize attacks as prescribed by infiltration doctrine. Once stopped, the Marines were able to put the Germans on the defensive, although German counterattacks to regain lost ground at Hill 142 and in Belleau Wood did feature artillery preparation and infiltration tactics. The Marine response to the infiltration was to contract their lines and hunt down the separated German units. At Cantigny, the German defenses crumpled during the initial attack and repeated counterattacks, preceded by artillery support, were unsuccessful at dislodging the American defenders. This pattern also repeated itself at Bouresches.

THE FRENCH

By May 1918, the French Army, like the British, was increasingly fragile. The French were still recovering from the mutinies of 1917 and both Foch and Pétain recognized that they were incapable of sustained offensive actions. In response to the German offensives in May, 1918, the

French divisions, averaging only 6,000 men, relied on large amounts of artillery support. The French artillery was able to blunt but not stop the German advance, allowing time for reinforcements to be brought up. French commanders fed these reinforcements into the battle without regard for coordination. Although French infantry supported both flanks of the 2nd Division, they demonstrated an inability to advance in conjunction with the American counterattacks.

French artillery was instrumental in supporting the initial attack on Cantigny, and supplemented American batteries in the struggle for Belleau Wood. While the French boasted of air superiority, American recollections note an absence of French air cover and that German air observation was unhindered throughout the battle for Belleau Wood.

ORDERS OF BATTLE

AMERICAN ARMY

2nd Division – Gen Bundy
4th Machine Gun Battalion
2nd Engineers Regiment
1st Field Signal Battalion

2nd Field Artillery Brigade – Gen Chamberlaine
    12th Field Artillery Regiment
    15th Field Artillery Regiment
    17th Field Artillery Regiment
    2nd Trench Mortar Battery

3rd Brigade – Gen Lewis
    5th Machine Gun Battalion

    23rd Infantry Regiment – Col Malone
        1st Battalion
        2nd Battalion
        3rd Battalion

    9th Infantry Regiment – Col Upton
        1st Battalion
        2nd Battalion
        3rd Battalion

4th Brigade – Brig Gen Harbord
    6th Machine Gun Battalion

    5th Marine Regiment – Colonel Neville
        1st Battalion
        2nd Battalion
        3rd Battalion

    6th Marine Regiment – Col Catlin
        1st Battalion
        2nd Battalion
        3rd Battalion

GERMAN ARMY

IV Reserve Corps – Gen von Conta

231st Division – GenLt von Hulsen

231st Infantry Brigade – Obst von Fischer
    442nd Infantry Regiment
    443rd Infantry Regiment
    444th Infantry Regiment

3rd Guard Reserve Field Artillery Regiment
    90th Foot Artillery Battalion

237th Division – GenLt von Jacobi

244th Infantry Brigade – GenMaj Pohlmann
    460th Infantry Regiment
    461st Infantry Regiment
    462nd Infantry Regiment

    83rd Field Artillery Regiment
    23rd Field Artillery (Detachment)

10th Division – GenLt von Gruter

    20th Infantry Brigade – Obst Sydow
        6th Grenadier Regiment
        47th Infantry Regiment
        398th Infantry Regiment

    56th Field Artillery Regiment
    11th Field Artillery (Detachment)

28th Division – GenMaj Bohn

    55th Infantry Brigade
        40th Fusilier Regiment
        109th Grenadier Regiment
        110th Grenadier Regiment

    14th Field Artillery Regiment
    55th Foot Artillery Battalion

197th Division – GenLt Wilhemi

    210th Infantry Brigade – Obst von
        Sachsen-Meiningen
        273rd Reserve Infantry Regiment
        7th Saxon Jäger Regiment
        28th Ersatz Infantry Regiment

    261st Field Artillery Regiment

5th Guard Division – GenMaj von Haxthausen

    2nd Guard Brigade
        3rd Guard Foot Regiment
        3rd Guard Grenadier Regiment
        20th Infantry Regiment

        4th Guard Field Artillery Regiment
        1st Guard Reserve Foot Artillery
    (Detachment)

OPPOSING PLANS

GERMAN PLANS

Operation *Blücher* had been intended by Ludendorff as a feint, designed to draw French reserves away from support of the British Army. Operations *Michael* and *Georgette* had rattled the British in Flanders, and threatened British access to the Channel ports. The German attack against Gen Duchene's French Sixth Army across the Chemin des Dames succeeded beyond all expectations, tempting the German High Command to abandon their original plans to shift their offensive back to the British in Flanders. The Germans correctly observed that the French seemed incapable of stopping their drive towards Paris. With forces only 40 miles from the French capital, Ludendorff and his staff convinced themselves that the potential of capturing Paris was worth the change in plans. Complicating matters was the introduction of American forces, which allowed the French to stem the German advance without withdrawing significant resources from the British.

When German forces slammed into American forces only 35 miles from Paris, Ludendorff suspended the offensive, leaving the German forces in a deep salient that would be difficult to defend. Ludendorff organized Operation *Gneisenau,* designed to draw more French reserves and improve his position in the salient. *Gneisenau* began on June 9, with von Hutier's Eighteenth Army advancing 6 miles, but was stopped on June 11, 1918, when the French Tenth Army attacked the German left flank. By that time the momentum of the war had shifted to the Allies. By the end of June, as the Americans were clearing the last sections of Belleau Wood, the momentum of the war had shifted again. Ludendorff was never able to resume his original strategy and from that point onward the Allies would dictate the direction of the war.

AMERICAN PLANS

As Ludendorff was planning Operation *Blücher* the Americans were continuing their intense regime of training. At the same time, Foch was trying to determine where best to deploy the American forces made available by Pershing. The Allies suspected that Ludendorff would attack the French in an effort to draw forces south from support of the British. The American 1st Division was deployed in the Picardy area in anticipation of the next German offensive. It was expected that the Americans would be on the flank of the German thrust but, as Allied intelligence determined that the German attack would be further south against the French on the Aisne, Pershing and his staff developed plans to capture Cantigny. Operation *Blücher* was launched on May 27,

7th Machine Gun Battalion marching towards Château-Thierry, May 31, 1918.

French Char Schneider tank. Introduced in late 1916 and armed with a 75mm cannon and Hotchkiss machine guns, this tank supported the American assault on Cantigny.

limiting the French artillery support available for the Cantigny attack. The Cantigny attack and subsequent battle dragged on for several days, limiting the availability of the 1st Division for further operations.

Operation *Blücher* tore open the French front and required the immediate deployment of the American 2nd and 3rd Divisions. Gen Foch announced that he was unconcerned about the German attack, maintaining that as long as he held the shoulders of the salient he could counterattack and stop the German drive. Despite Foch's reassuring words, the French commanders on the ground were in a state of panic and recognized the seriousness of the situation. French units were melting away in the face of the German attack and Paris was at risk.

At the urgent request of the French, the 3rd Division blocked the German advance at Château-Thierry, while the 2nd Division stemmed the German tide near Champillon. While the Germans were stopped they still threatened Paris, and communications with Metz and Verdun. French Gen Degoutte ordered the Americans to go over to the offensive on June 5, 1918. Overly confident after their repulse of the German attack, Gen Bundy and Harbord readily agreed. Rather than request time to gather adequate intelligence and reorganize their commands, Bundy and Harbord began planning for the American counterattack. A three-phase plan of attack was quickly developed. The first phase of the attack would capture Hill 142, which dominated the surrounding countryside, then drive through Belleau Wood from the west and south, emerging from the wood to capture Bouresches and the high ground beyond.

Neither side planned to fight at Belleau Wood. The Germans and Americans were drawn into the struggle for Belleau Wood for different reasons. Strategically unimportant, the outcome of the battle would have long-term impact for both sides.

AMERICA ENTERS THE WAR

Gen Pershing sailed for Europe at the end of May, 1917, with a staff of 58 officers, including two Marines and George S. Patton. He was greeted in England by Prime Minister Lloyd George and appointed to "command all the land forces of the United States operating in continental Europe and in the United Kingdom of Great Britain and Ireland, including any part of the Marine Corps which may be detached for service there with the army."

Pershing had been given direct orders from President Wilson to "cooperate with the forces of the other countries employed against the enemy, but the underlying idea must be kept in view that the forces of the United States are a separate and distinct component of the combined forces." After hearing Pershing's proposals to establish an independent American Army rather than integrate combat units in the English and French armies, the British suggested that they would not be able to provide shipping for American forces given their own needs.

Pershing arrived in France on June 13, 1917. During the first half of 1917 the war had taken an ominous turn for the French. In April, 1917, the new French Commander-in-Chief, Robert Nivelle, initiated a disastrous offensive on the Chemin des Dames, costing the French the loss of 187,000 men in just ten days. On April 29, a French unit refused to follow orders and the mutiny spread quickly to other units. Nivelle was relieved and Henri Pétain, who had been dismissed just a year before, was appointed in his place. A total of 23,000 French soldiers were tried by courts martial, 400 sentenced to death, and 50 shot. Although Pétain's quick actions avoided the complete collapse of the French Army, it was a spent force, unable to mount offensive actions.

Responding to pleas from French Marshal Joseph Joffre for a visible show of support, the hastily assembled 1st Division sailed in June, 1917, along with the 5th Marine Regiment. The 6th Marine Regiment sailed later in the year, landing in France in October. Prior to the arrival of the 6th Regiment, the War Department authorized the combination of the 5th and 6th Marine Regiments, joined by the 6th Marine Machine Gun Battalion, to create the 4th Brigade. In late October the 4th Brigade was assigned to join the Army's 3rd Brigade to form the 2nd Division. Additional American units, including the 3rd, 26th, and 42nd divisions, trickled into France throughout late 1917 and early 1918.

Pershing and his staff spent the summer of 1917 organizing the infrastructure necessary to support the establishment of the American Army. At the end of June, Pershing and his staff had come to the conclusion that US forces should be centered in the Lorraine region of France, providing direct lines of communication and supply with the Atlantic coast ports, supplemented by the Mediterranean port of Marseilles. Although the American units were not yet ready to undertake

Men of the 5th Marine Regiment disembarking in France in June, 1917. Note that at this time the Marines still wore canvas leggings rather than puttees. Also note the bugler in the center of the picture.

any offensive actions, Pershing's staff had already begun to draw up plans to use their deployment in Lorraine as a springboard to attack the St Mihiel salient.

Pershing dispatched his Marine regiment to oversee security at the ports, ordered the 1st Division to Gondrecourt, and moved his general headquarters staff from Paris to Chaumont. A staff college was established at Langres, 40 miles south of Chaumont. Time constraints meant that the four-month training cycle planned for each American division prior to combat was completed only by the 1st Division.

As the Americans settled down to begin their training regime in the fall and winter of 1917, the Allied cause suffered a series of hammer blows. First, the Russian Revolution of October led inexorably to Russia entering into a separate peace with Germany, freeing up thousands of German troops for service in the West. In the fall, the Austrians inflicted a crushing blow on the Italians at Caporetto. On December 22, 1917, Gen Pétain issued a pessimistic message to the French Army:

> *The Entente will not recover superiority in manpower until the American Army is capable of placing in line a certain number of large units: until then, we must, under the penalty of irremediable attrition maintain a waiting attitude, with the idea firmly placed in mind of resuming as soon as we can, the offensive which alone will bring us ultimate victory.*

By May, 1918, the American Army had established a small presence in the structure of the combined Allied forces on the Western Front. The 1st, 2nd, 26th, and 42nd divisions formed the core of the American Army, but even among these core divisions the level of training and effectiveness varied widely. The 1st, 2nd, and 26th divisions had been through only elementary training under French tutelage. These divisions had also been deployed for short periods in quiet sectors and subjected to heavy artillery bombardment, which included gas and periodic trench raids. The Germans, having identified the American troops during these deployments, were instructed by Ludendorff and the general staff to increase their attacks and attempt to demoralize the Americans.

The opening of Operation *Georgette* caught the Americans in transition. The 1st Division had just completed the capture of Cantigny and the 2nd Division was making preparations to relieve the 1st Division. The 26th Division was deployed in the Toul sector, while the 42nd Division was in the Baccarat sector. The 3rd Division had arrived in France in March, 1918, and was still completing its initial deployment in the Chateauvillain sector. The engineering elements of the 3rd Division had been assigned to the British Fifth Army on the Somme.

FIRST BLOOD

The first Americans killed in action were two men from the 11th Engineers, assigned to the British 3rd Army at Goureaucourt, killed by artillery fire, September 5, 1917. On October 21, the 1st Division entered the line at Bathelemont, attached to the French 18th Division. Pershing's plan called for a battalion from each of the four infantry regiments, with a machine-gun company and attached engineer and signal elements, to occupy a sector for ten days. American officers would retain control over their companies but battalion and regimental officers would observe while the French remained in overall control.

The 7th Bavarian Landwehr Regiment had suspicions that Americans were occupying the trenches opposite them. On the night of November 2–3, the Germans dropped a box barrage on Company F, 2nd Battalion, 16th Regiment, and 213 Bavarians rushed through the heavy fog and smoke into the American outposts. When they withdrew, three Americans were dead, five wounded, and 12 captured. German losses were two dead, seven wounded, and one deserter. The commander of the raid reported that "the enemy was very good in hand-to-hand fighting…"

Although the French rejected requests from the 1st Division to launch a counterattack, Maj Theodore Roosevelt, son of former President Theodore Roosevelt, convinced Gen Bordeaux to allow his battalion to carry out an "embuscade." The major's brother, Lt Archie Roosevelt, also served in the 26th Regiment and was assigned to lead the raid. Despite meticulous planning, the unit became lost in no man's land and its French advisor directed it back over the strenuous objections of Lt

General John Pershing, commander of the American Army in France, with 1st Division commander General Bullard and his staff conducting a review of 1st Division units during summer, 1917. Pershing made no secret that the 1st Division was his favorite throughout the war.

Roosevelt. The action of Roosevelt's raiding party represented the first offensive action of any American unit in France.

The 1st Division completed its training in late November. Pershing, unhappy with the pace of training and lacking confidence in the competence of the 1st Division commander, Maj Gen William Sibert, appointed his aide, Gen Robert Bullard, in his place. 1st Division was ordered to join the French 69th Division in early January, 1918, in the Ansauville area of the Toul sector, 40 miles north of Gondrecourt. In early February, Bullard and his staff were given new directives on establishing defensive positions. These changes were the result of the capture of German documents outlining the training underway in the German Army, based on the maneuver of rupture.

In late February, the 1st Division also experienced the first major use of poison gas. The 3rd Battalion of the 18th Regiment lost eight dead and 77 wounded as a result. Throughout February and March, the Germans and Americans traded trench raids. On April 3, 1918, the 1st Division turned over their positions to the 26th Division. During their tour in the Ansauville area they had suffered 549 casualties.

By early 1918, the 1st, 2nd, 26th, and 42nd divisions formed the core of the American Army in France. The 2nd Division and 42nd Division were assigned to quiet sectors in Lorraine, while the 26th was placed in Chemin des Dames. The 42nd Division began its stint in the front lines, in the Luneville sector, in late February, 1918.

2nd Division

The 2nd Division was unique among American combat divisions, composed of the 3rd Brigade, made up of US regular army units, the 9th and 23rd regiments, and the 4th Brigade, which included the 5th and 6th Marine regiments. The division was commanded by Gen Omar Bundy. By June, 1918, Pershing had begun to have his doubts about Bundy's ability to lead the 2nd Division. Pershing commented in his diary on June 9, 1918 that he would "relieve him at the first opportunity."

The 3rd Brigade was led by Brig Gen Edward Lewis and the 4th Brigade by Brig Gen James Harbord. The 2nd Division was assigned to Lorraine, near Sommedieue, and entered the trenches in mid-March.

Men from the 18th Regiment in the trenches, February, 1918.

German suspicions that the Americans had entered the trenches were confirmed in late March, when they found the body of an officer from the 9th Regiment. The admissions of a captured French soldier that an American battalion had arrived led the commander of the German 82nd Reserve Division to increase patrols and artillery barrages.

The Germans began organizing a large-scale raid in early April. Raiding parties from the three regiments of the 82nd Reserve Division were combined with support elements from the 272nd Reserve Regiment. The attack group, totaling over 650 men, would be supported by 12 artillery batteries. The Germans selected the area opposite Rouvrois for the attack. German artillery activity steadily increased, leading French officers to warn the Americans that a large-scale German raid might be expected against the 3rd Battalion, 23rd Regiment, which held the Bois de Bouchot. Col Malone, 23rd Regiment commander, ordered his battalion commanders to have their men sleep on their arms.

Maizey Raid

At 2300hrs on April 13, 1918, the Germans laid a box barrage on areas defended by the 9th Regiment near Maizey. The barrage continued until about 0030hrs. When the men of the 9th Regiment emerged from

their dugouts they found the Germans from the 270th, 271st, and 272nd regiments swarming around their positions.

Survivors from the 9th Regiment reported that 30 or more Germans dressed as French surgeons with Red Cross armbands had approached the American lines. Although challenged, they explained they had been treating the wounded from a French patrol. Having gained entry to the first line trenches they overpowered the sentries. They then cut two lanes through the wire, allowing two companies of storm troopers to advance against the support positions.

The Germans penetrated the American lines at several points, and one German unit reached the rear areas. Companies L and I were the focus of the German attack, and for over two hours a desperate hand-to-hand struggle was waged within the barrage. At about 0200hrs the Germans began to withdraw, taking with them prisoners and equipment. The retiring Germans were caught in an American artillery counter-barrage, which allowed many of the American prisoners to overpower their guards and escape. The American 9th Regiment lost seven killed, 39 wounded, and 25 captured. The Germans left behind 60 dead and 11 captured, taking away their wounded. Several of the German impostors were captured and executed the next morning with grenades.

The Germans and 2nd Division continued to trade small raids throughout April and early May, 1918. These raids included several appearances of a special raiding force known as "Hindenburg's Traveling Circus," that was to attack the 26th Division at Seicheprey. On May 15 the division was reassigned to Gisors Chaumont-en-Vexin, west of Paris and directly in the path of the latest German offensive.

Seicheprey Raid

Within a week of 26th Division replacing 1st Division the Germans launched a series of raids. The 104th Regiment repulsed a German raid

When the Whine of "Kamrad!" Lifts Above the Clamor **by Frank Schoonover. Illustration from** *Ladies Home Journal,* **1918. During the course of the attacks on villages such as Cantigny, Bouresches, and Vaux, the preliminary artillery barrage drove most of the defenders into cover in buildings and cellars. The rapid advance of American troops resulted in large numbers of Germans being captured in their hiding places. (Courtesy of Delaware National Guard)**

on April 10 and turned back two simultaneous attacks two days later. Not satisfied with their probes, the Germans launched a full-scale raid against companies C and D, 1st Battalion, 102nd Regiment, in the early morning of April 20. After a two-hour barrage, under the cover of an early morning fog, an estimated 2,800 German storm troopers belonging to the 259th Infantry reinforced by "Hindenburg's Traveling Circus," overran the two companies. Throughout the day the situation remained confused. The captain of Company C stumbled into battalion headquarters to report his command wiped out.

Several patrols were sent forward and found the remnants of the two companies engaged in desperate hand-to-hand fighting. A planned counterattack was aborted when the company commander refused to carry out the assault. By the time the confusion was sorted out the Germans had withdrawn, leaving 100 survivors of companies C and D. The Americans reported 669 casualties, including 81 killed and 187 captured or missing. The Germans admitted to c.600 casualties, while the Americans claimed to have inflicted twice that many casualties on their attackers.

The scale of the Seicheprey attack and American losses were magnified as a result of the continuing debate about the deployment of the American Army. American losses and confusion at Seicheprey allowed the British and French to openly question the Americans' fighting ability. The repercussions of the Seicheprey raid hung heavy over Pershing and his command as the 1st Division was given orders to capture the village of Cantigny.

CANTIGNY

The 1st Division was deployed in the Montdidier sector on April 24, 1918, and placed under the command of the VI Corps, First French Army. The German High Command had given orders that whenever American units were discovered in front-line positions they were to be subjected to

intense attacks, in an attempt to discourage this yet-untested army. After their deployment, the 1st Division was the target of repeated artillery attacks that included gas. As the Americans settled into their new positions the French began to rotate several of their divisions out of the front lines. On May 5, overall command of the sector was transferred to the French X Corps.

When the anticipated German offensive failed to materialize in mid-May, the 1st Division was given orders to prepare to capture the village of Cantigny. Cantigny afforded the Germans an unrestricted view of a large portion of the American positions and screened German rear areas. The attack on Cantigny would represent the first large-scale American offensive of the war. For several weeks the Americans strengthened their positions, planned the operation, and rehearsed the attack.

The 28th Infantry Regiment, commanded by Col Hansen Ely, was selected to lead the assault. Ely, a West Point graduate, embodied the tough, aggressive officer that Pershing demanded. The plan of attack developed by Lt Col George Marshall, directed the 3/28th to advance on the left, securing the Cantigny–Grivesnes ridge road and establishing contact with the French to the north. The 2/28th was assigned the task of carrying Cantigny with the assistance of 12 French tanks and a platoon of flamethrowers.

Two companies of the 1/28th were ordered to skirt the southern edge of Cantigny and take up positions to cover Fontaine-sous-Montdidier.

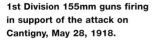

1st Division 155mm guns firing in support of the attack on Cantigny, May 28, 1918.

Another company of the 1/28th would block the southern flank. Marshall attached a machine-gun company to each battalion and an engineer company to support the overall attack. The 28th Regiment was also buttressed by elements of the 16th and 18th regiments, including additional machine guns, Stokes mortars, and 37mm guns. Marshall's meticulous planning was noted by Pershing, who would later reassign him to his headquarters to head up operational planning for the entire army. In World War II Marshall would rise to become the first American five-star general and oversee all American armed forces.

Significant French artillery support was also provided to the Americans. The French committed 84 75mm guns, 12 155mm guns, and 12 220mm mortars. One group of 17 75mm guns was assigned to provide a rolling barrage to cover the advance, while another group of 15 75mm guns would fire in support of both flanks. The 155mm guns would both support the assault and be available for counter-battery fire. Taking a cue from the innovative artillery tactics of the Germans, the preparatory barrage was planned to be short and intense, reaching its maximum intensity for just five minutes prior to the assault. It was to be followed by a rolling barrage designed to precede the infantry assault. Guns firing gas shells were assigned to pummel artillery concentrations and assembly areas well behind the German line of defense.

In preparation for the attack, Gen Bullard reorganized each platoon, decreasing their size from 50 to 40 men and creating a fifth platoon in each company. Bullard originally planned on retaining the fifth platoon as the nucleus for reconstituting the companies in the event of high casualties. Criticism of the revised organization from Pershing's staff resulted in the fifth platoons participating in the attack as carrying parties, bringing extra ammunition, water, and equipment.

During the night of May 22, the 28th Regiment was withdrawn from their positions and sent to a secure rear area to rehearse the attack. After two full rehearsals Bullard deemed the 28th Regiment ready and set the morning of May 28 for the attack.

Cantigny was defended by the German 82nd Reserve Division. The 270th Regiment was deployed north of the village, in front of the Bois de Lalval. The 272nd Regiment occupied the center of the divisional front, with its left flank resting on the edge of Cantigny. The 271st Regiment occupied the village and extended back to Hill 104. The German regiments deployed one battalion forward and a second battalion sheltered in wooded areas as a reserve. Their 3rd battalions were sent several miles to the rear.

American staff became alarmed several days before the attack when an American lieutenant, carrying maps of the location of American ammunition and supply dumps, was captured. More ominously, the day before the attack the Germans launched a series of raids against the American positions. One raid, carried out by three platoons of German shock troops, struck the 26th Regiment in Bois de Fontaine. While the Americans repulsed the attack, the Germans captured one soldier. The other raid, by elements of the 272nd Regiment, was directed against the 2/28th, which had just returned to the line in preparation for the attack on Cantigny. Again, the Germans ran into a determined American defense and were driven back. The interrogation of captured Germans convinced Bullard and his staff that the Germans did not suspect an

RIGHT *Cantigny: Where the Americans Won Their First Laurels* by Frank Schoonover. Illustration from *Ladies Home Journal*, 1918, showing the American assault on Cantigny. American infantry is shown battling through the ruins of the village, supported by French Schneider tanks and French planes. (Courtesy of Delaware National Guard)

ASSAULT ON CANTIGNY

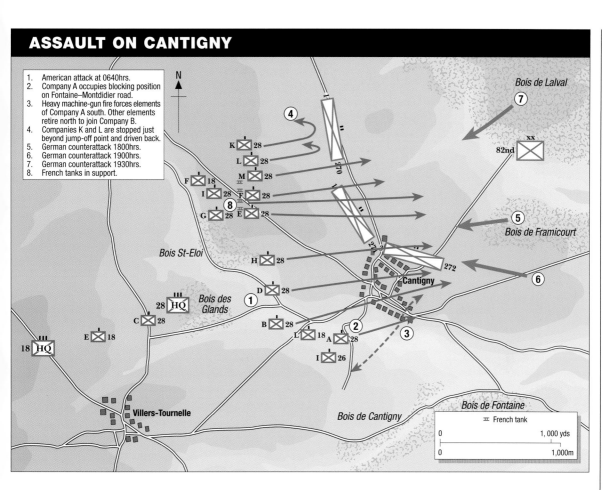

1. American attack at 0640hrs.
2. Company A occupies blocking position on Fontaine–Montdidier road.
3. Heavy machine-gun fire forces elements of Company A south. Other elements retire north to join Company B.
4. Companies K and L are stopped just beyond jump-off point and driven back.
5. German counterattack 1800hrs.
6. German counterattack 1900hrs.
7. German counterattack 1930hrs.
8. French tanks in support.

Bois de Lalval

Bois de Framicourt

Bois St-Eloi

Cantigny

Bois des Glands

Villers-Tournelle

Bois de Cantigny

Bois de Fontaine

French tank

0   1,000 yds

0   1,000m

German Private Feldpausch, captured by the 1st Division during a raid on May 27, 1918. Interrogation of Private Feldpausch and other prisoners convinced General Bullard that the Germans were unaware of the impending American attack on Cantigny.

attack and their purpose was to divert American attention while they rotated their front-line units.

Despite lingering concerns over the possibility that the Germans had learned about the attack, the American 28th Regiment, augmented by the French tanks and flamethrower detachments, jumped off at 0645hrs on May 28. All three battalions of the 28th Regiment were deployed in line for the attack, with each battalion arrayed in three lines. Engineer and machine-gun companies were attached to the assault battalions. Each American soldier carried 220 rounds of rifle ammunition, two hand grenades and one rifle grenade, four sand bags, and a shovel or pick. Following close behind the rolling barrage the 28th moved across no man's land quickly, pushing aside feeble German resistance, and occupied Cantigny by 0730hrs. The American plan was to advance under a mile beyond the village and establish a strong defensive line.

The American attack caught the Germans in the midst of a relief of units, and many men had taken refuge from the artillery barrage in the cellars of the village. The rolling barrage all but destroyed the 1st and 2nd companies of the 271st Regiment and the 12th Company of the 272nd Regiment. The Americans advanced close behind their barrage and captured the remaining Germans as they emerged. Although several of the Schneider tanks broke down during the advance, the mere appearance of the remaining tanks added to the panic among the defenders. The Americans moved quickly, leaving the French flamethrower units to root out the remaining pockets of resistance.

The capture of Cantigny cost the Americans fewer than 100 casualties, while capturing over 180 Germans. The 2nd Battalion moved east of Cantigny and immediately began to consolidate and strengthen their positions, digging entrenchments and stringing barbed wire against the expected German counterattack. Ely's men established three strongpoints, which followed an arc beginning with the cemetery on the north, through a small patch of woods northeast of the town, to Château Cantigny on the southwest. Each strongpoint was defended by a platoon of infantry. These positions were further strengthened with two machine guns and captured German Maxim heavy machine guns.

While the 2/28th in the center enjoyed success, the 1/28th, covering the right flank south of Cantigny ran into heavy machine-gun fire. Ely sent Company L, 18th Regiment, to stiffen the 1st Battalion position. On the left, north of Cantigny, the 3/28th also found itself exposed to heavy machine-gun fire. The German fire had disrupted Company K's advance just beyond the American barbed wire and driven Company L south into Company M. 3/28th Battalion Commander Maj Cullison responded by committing his reserve, Company I, which joined the remnants of Company L in the cemetery.

By noon, the Germans brought up machine guns and their artillery began to fall along the American positions, driving the defenders into shell holes and hastily dug trenches.

Although French artillery had provided strong initial support, the need to restore the line destroyed by the German offensive over the Chemin des Dames resulted in orders to withdraw their batteries. The loss of French artillery put the Americans in a precarious position.

With reduced French artillery available to respond to the increasing German barrages, the Americans struggled to repulse several probes of

their lines throughout the early afternoon. During this period French aerial reconnaissance and American observers reported pockets of Germans organizing for counterattacks. Ely and his staff called for interdiction fire from the remaining artillery.

The first serious counterattack was launched by the German 82nd Division at 1200hrs and then again at 1845hrs. Elements of the 2nd and 3rd Battalions, 272nd Regiment advanced out of the Bois de Framicourt. In the center, the 2nd/271st moved down from Hill 104 towards Cantigny and 2nd/83rd Regiment advanced along the Cantigny–Fontaine road.

The Germans failed to coordinate their advance with artillery support, and their infantry fell 200 yards behind the rolling barrage, allowing the Americans to recover and shatter the attack. While the first German waves were cut down by American rifles, the 1st Division artillery responded with a counterbarrage that decimated the succeeding waves.

At the end of May 28, the Americans clung precariously to their hold on Cantigny. Ely continued to feed his reserves into battle, particularly along the southern flank to strengthen the 3/28th. He committed his last reserve company and three companies of the 18th Regiment to strengthen that portion of his line.

On May 29, the battle turned into a desperate slugging match. Twice in the early morning depleted elements of the 272nd Regiment, buttressed by a company from the 270th Regiment, launched attacks out of Bois de Framicourt. Both attacks failed to make headway. Von Hutier organized another attack for the late afternoon by the 83rd Regiment of the 25th Reserve Division, supported by a heavy artillery barrage. American artillery, now focused on breaking up the German attacks rather than disabling their batteries, assisted in stopping the German assault. Although the German infantry had made no gains, the shelling from German artillery began to take its toll on the 28th Regiment. After conferring with Col Parker of the 18th Regiment, Col Ely requested immediate support and relief. Bullard rejected the request but promised the 28th Regiment would be relieved as soon as possible.

On May 30, the Germans continued to pound the 28th Regiment with artillery but von Hutier, now convinced that the Americans were not

DEFENSE OF CANTIGNY, MAY 28, 1918 (pages 36–37)
Early on May 28, 1918 the 28th Regiment of the 1st Division launched an attack on the village of Cantigny. The attack, meticulously planned and rehearsed, was the first major American offensive action of the war. The preliminary American artillery bombardment drove the German defenders into their shelters. The Americans, advancing close behind a creeping barrage and supported by several French Schneider tanks and flamethrower teams, quickly overran the 3/272nd Reserve Regiment, capturing scores and driving the remainder into the Bois de Framicourt.

Consistent with their pre-assault planning the Americans quickly advanced beyond the village and set up defensive positions. The Americans carried with them entrenching equipment (1) and barbed wire. While the Germans organized their counterattack the Americans prepared strongpoints in the rubble and strung wire (2).

Although the Germans were slow to react to the capture of Cantigny, by early evening they began a series of counterattacks, intending to recapture the village. At approximately 1830hrs, following a preliminary bombardment, the 2/271st Reserve Regiment rushed out of the Bois de Framicourt and attacked the 2/28th Regiment defending positions east of Cantigny. As officers directed their fire (3) the American infantry concentrated deliberate rifle fire on the Germans attacking out of the Bois de Framicourt (4). The Americans were supported by Chauchat light machine guns (5) and a captured German Maxim machine gun (6). The Chauchat was supported by an assistant gunner carrying extra ammunition (7). German artillery fire supporting the attack was weak and ineffective and the German infantry fell behind their barrage (8). In response, American artillery fired a box barrage that isolated the advance elements of the German attack (9) from support. The Americans fought off several disjointed German counterattacks throughout May 28, 1918. For the next several days the 28th Regiment suffered from galling artillery fire, and determined German counterattacks but held the village, suffering over 900 killed and wounded before being relieved on May 31, 1918.

Interrogation of German prisoners captured at Cantigny. Note the variety of uniforms, some wearing puttees, and the relative youth of several of the Germans.

intent on advancing towards Montdidier, was disposed to wait. On the night of May 30–31, Bullard released the 16th Regiment from reserve and directed them to replace the 28th Regiment and elements of the 18th Regiment defending Cantigny.

The securing of Cantigny cost the 1st Division over 900 killed and wounded. The German 82nd Reserve Division had lost over 1,400 men, including 285 captured by the Americans, while the 83rd Regiment of the 25th Reserve Division reported 324 killed.

While Cantigny was of very little tactical value and no strategic importance, its impact on American confidence, especially after the debacle of Seicheprey, was significant. More importantly, the success at Cantigny was intended to convey a message to the French and British that the Americans could be relied upon to shoulder their share of the burden. To the Germans, Cantigny was an ominous precursor of the growing American challenge to German moral ascendancy over the battlefield.

The defense of Cantigny also provided the Americans with an important combat experience. Only hours after his troops had been withdrawn from their defensive positions, Col Ely wrote:

> *The great strain on men holding a front line trench or being practically*
> *without sleep for three or four days and nights seriously weakens*
> *them; and when there is added to this casualties amounting in some*
> *companies as high as 40 percent, with casualties among company officers*
> *of infantry companies of from 33 percent to 100 percent, it is believed*
> *that as soon as a force has gained and fairly consolidated its objective,*
> *having suffered such losses … it should be relieved by fresh troops.*

While Ely's conclusions were sound, the coming struggle over Belleau Wood would require the American High Command to learn these lessons over again on a much larger scale.

OPERATION *BLÜCHER*

With the conclusion of the German Operation *Georgette* on April 29, the Allies spent the early part of May reassessing their positions. Ludendorff still believed that he could defeat the British in Flanders, but in order to do so he needed to draw French reserves away from the north. He decided upon an offensive, codenamed *Blücher*, to be focused against the Chemin des Dames along the Aisne River. Foch and his staff began planning for a counterattack designed to support the British and recapture the ground lost since March. The French High Command became convinced that the Germans, having drawn attention to the north, would return to expand the salient they created during Operation *Michael*.

With an eye towards attacking the southern flank of the anticipated German push, Foch began moving additional forces along this line. This included the American 1st Division, which had been relieved by the 26th Division from positions opposite Mont Sec and moved to positions west of Montdidier, near the village of Cantigny. The French staff expected the German offensive to begin about May 18, and the 1st Division was positioned to advance in conjunction with a French division on either flank. French intelligence was baffled when May 18 came and went and the Germans gave no indication that they would renew their attacks. Foch and his staff failed to appreciate the ability of the Germans to quickly shift their offensives from one sector to another. An American intelligence officer, Capt Samuel Hubbard, reviewed the evidence and concluded that the next German effort would be in the direction of Paris, across the Chemin des Dames, at the end of May. Not surprisingly, the French staff dismissed Hubbard's prediction.

Gen Duchene, commander of the French Sixth Army, which included six French and four British divisions, was responsible for holding the Chemin des Dames ridge. Duchene and his staff rejected both the directives to deploy in depth and the warnings of an impending attack. On May 25, a group of French soldiers, recently escaped from German captivity, reported large concentrations of German infantry and artillery on the other side. On May 26, two captured Germans revealed that a general attack would begin after midnight. The skeptical interrogators did not pass along their findings until mid-afternoon and the staff at Duchene's Sixth Army Headquarters dismissed the report as unverified rumor.

On May 27, Ludendorff launched Operation *Blücher*, crossing the Aisne River and driving a 12-mile wedge in the French lines between Soissons and Reims. In the early morning of May 27, 17 German divisions poured over the Chemin des Dames, destroying the 21st and 22nd divisions of Duchene's Sixth Army. French Prime Minister Clemenceau traveled to the front and sought out Duchene, who told him there was nothing to stop the Germans but *"de la poussiere"* – mere dust.

Three days later the Germans were on the Marne River, less than 50 miles from Paris. As the German advance pushed aside feeble French resistance, Foch maintained that the attack was a mere feint designed to draw French reserves from Flanders. Foch ordered French forces to maintain strong positions on either side of the salient created by the German attack. As the situation worsened, Foch informed Gen Haig that he was considering withdrawing the French forces that had been sent north to assist the British, and might have to request British help in the south. Despite maintaining strong positions astride the German advance, French resistance in the path of the Germans continued to collapse. The German 231st Division moved relentlessly towards Château-Thierry and a crossing of the Marne River.

As the German advance continued the French general staff grew more desperate. Col Fox Conner, Pershing's chief of operations, reported that the French were urging the immediate deployment of American divisions at the front. Responding to an urgent request from Gen Ragueneau of the French Military Mission for assistance, Conner ordered the American 3rd Division to Château-Thierry.

CHÂTEAU-THIERRY AND BELLEAU WOOD

CHÂTEAU-THIERRY

The lead element of the 3rd Division, the 7th Machine Gun Battalion commanded by Maj James Taylor, arrived near Château-Thierry in the early afternoon of May 31. Capt Charles H. Houghton, commanding the lead elements of the battalion, made his way across the main bridge over the Marne, connecting the south bank to an island in the river and then to the north bank. A second bridge, east of the island, carried the railroad over the Marne. The French 10th Colonial Division was slowly retiring along the north bank towards the bridges. The French were commanded by Gen Marchand, who ordered Houghton to deploy his machine guns along the northern bank of the island and south of the railroad bridge to cover the retreating French forces. One section of American machine guns from Company A, two guns and 12 men, commanded by Lt John Bissell, deployed with a French unit north of the railroad bridge. By 1600hrs the American units were in position as the French prepared both bridges for demolition. During the night the remainder of the 7th Machine Gun Battalion guns were deployed in the houses facing the river or in the gardens between the buildings.

At 0400hrs on June 1, the German 231st Division began a methodical advance through the northern sections of Château-Thierry, pushing

7th Machine Gun Battalion detraining at Montmirail on their way to Château-Thierry.

back the French defenders, intent on crossing the Marne. The French retired towards the safety of the west bridge. As night approached a small group of French, supported by the American machine-gun batteries, vigorously defended the northern end of the bridge against growing German pressure. At 2230hrs the French blew up the west bridge while the American machine guns swept the northern bank.

Lt Bissell and his unit were trapped and forced to retire towards the railroad bridge. As they retreated the American guns paused, allowing them to cross. During the lull a small group of Germans also crossed the bridge but were quickly hunted down and captured.

By dawn on June 2, the Germans had occupied the length of the north bank and directed intense artillery fire across the river. The Americans and French strengthened their positions, despite the increasing artillery and small arms fire. German snipers on the north bank also added to the danger. At 2100hrs the Germans attempted to cross the railroad bridge, but were driven back with heavy losses. The avenues leading to the bridge became killing zones and when German casualties mounted the attack was called off. The remaining elements of the American 3rd Division moved up to reinforce Château-Thierry on June 4, relieving the depleted French units along the south bank of the Marne. The German drive to cross the Marne was stopped.

With their original line of advance blocked, the Germans shifted their energy to the west, directing the 10th Reserve and 237th divisions across Clignon Brook and through Bouresches, Belleau, Torcy, and Bussiares.

BELLEAU WOOD

Advance to Battle

The American 2nd Division had originally been assigned to the French VII Corps, and was scheduled to relieve the American 1st Division around Cantigny, but with the increased German pressure in the direction of Château-Thierry the division was transferred to Gen Degoutte's battered XXI Corps, composed of Gen Michel's 43rd Division and Gen Gaucher's 164th Division.

In the late afternoon of May 30, a French staff officer sought a hurried interview with Col Preston Brown, 2nd Division Chief of Staff. Brown

View of destroyed west bridge across the Meuse River, looking towards the north bank.

American machine-gun team deployed in the gardens between buildings on the south bank at Château-Thierry.

spoke fluent French, and provided principal coordination with French staff, whom he alternately charmed and outraged. The French officer announced that the 2nd Division had been assigned to the Sixth French Army. Trucks would be arriving within the hour to carry the American infantry to the front. Additional vehicles might be available later to carry the machine guns, engineers, and artillery, but the French made no commitment to a timetable. In fact the French transport did not show up until 0400hrs the following morning. The Americans were loaded into camion convoys and the first trucks rumbled forward at 0600hrs.

On May 31, the 2nd Division was ordered by Degoutte to move to Meaux and await further orders. American staff feared that Degoutte and the French were nearing collapse. The convoys passed long lines of civilian refugees, intermixed with dazed and despondent French soldiers. As the day wore on, the 2nd Division received no fewer than four separate directives from Degoutte, reflecting the confusion in the French general staff. 4th Brigade commander James Harbord and Col Brown conferred late on May 31, in the midst of growing frustration.

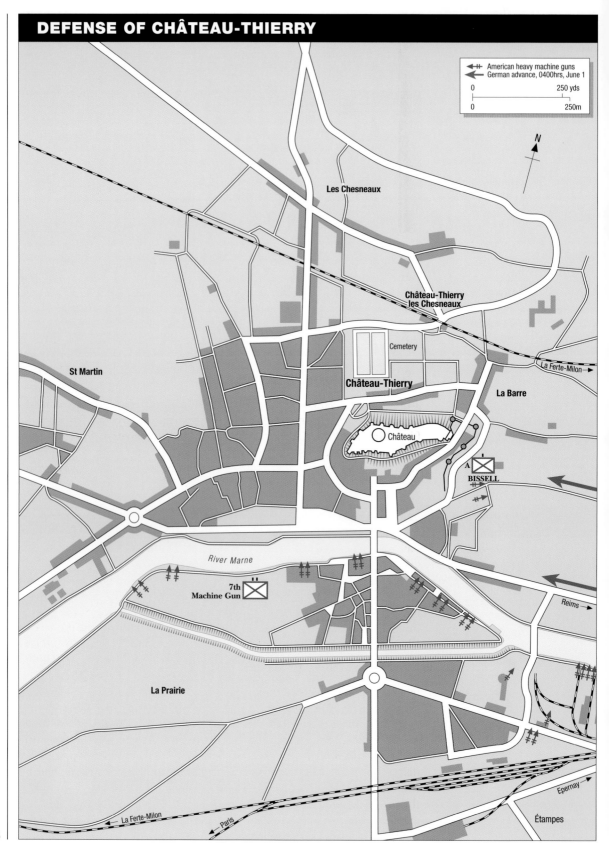

American heavy machine guns
German advance, 0400hrs, June 1

0   250 yds

0   250m

N

Les Chesneaux

Château-Thierry
les Chesneaux

Cemetery

La Ferte-Milon

St Martin

Château-Thierry

La Barre

Château

A
BISSELL

River Marne

7th
Machine Gun

Reims

La Prairie

La Ferte-Milon

Paris

Epernay

Étampes

Elements of the 3rd Division on the march to Château-Thierry, June 3, 1918.

Degoutte's final orders directed the 2nd Division to counter the German pressure building around Château-Thierry. The division was ordered to march towards Montreuil-aux-Lion. The 3rd Brigade, composed of the 9th and 23rd regiments, was to deploy north of the Paris–Metz highway. Harbord's 4th Brigade would deploy to the right of the 3rd Brigade, facing Vaux and Hill 204, with its headquarters at Bezu.

On May 31, the French Army Command concluded that the Germans were intent on opening the road to Paris at all costs. Their anxiety was heightened by the failure of their own planned counterattacks. The advance against Fismes had misfired. South of Soissons the attack of four divisions had gained little ground and was driven back. Elsewhere the German advance had continued unabated. The Germans captured the Nouvron plateau north of Soissons, and in the Ourcq River valley they pushed the French defenders back. Gen Pétain reported despondently that the reserves sent to stop the Germans had "melted away very quickly." British Gen Henry Wilson, who along with Haig had been in close communication with the French High Command throughout the crisis, wrote late on May 31, "Tomorrow will be a critical day. If Rupprecht now attacks south from Montdidier to Noyon and takes Compiègne the French Army is beaten."

During the night of May 31–June 1, Degoutte conferred with 2nd Division commander Gen Omar Bundy and Col Brown. The Americans found Degoutte pessimistic. He initially suggested that a general retreat might be in order, since the Germans had captured Hill 204, west of Château-Thierry, only four miles from his headquarters. He then quickly changed course and proposed an alternative strategy. Since the beginning of Operation *Blücher* the French had tried to plug the holes in their lines by shifting reserves and rushing them piecemeal into the breech, "where," as Gen Pétain had written to Gen Foch, "overwhelmed by numbers, they evaporated immediately, like drops of rain on a white hot iron." Despite its failings Degoutte proposed to follow that practice and commit the American units as they became available. Gen Bundy and Col Brown disagreed vehemently, arguing that the Americans had only rifles and 150 rounds of ammunition available. Bundy ended the discussion by stating that the American forces would not go into battle without their artillery and machine-gun units. The Americans suggested instead that their forces establish a defensive line through which the French could retreat and at

Traffic jams like this frustrated the efforts of the 2nd Division to move to the front. The instruments of the divisional band were carried in the wagons.

the same time stop the German advance. Once the advance was stopped the Americans would go over to the offensive. Degoutte gave his grudging approval to the American plan but expressed doubts about the fighting ability of the untested 2nd Division. "Gen Degoutte," replied Col Brown, "these are American regulars. In one hundred and fifty years they have never been beaten. They will hold."

As the American 2nd Division was trying to establish a defensive line, Foch and Pétain were conferring with Pershing about the need to open an attack on the flanks of the German penetration. The plan called for the German advance to be stopped along a line from Noyon to the Marne River and following the river to the east. Once the Germans were stopped, the French planned on attacking with 15–20 divisions from the east while another 15 divisions gathered around Châlons, and would attack to the northwest towards Reims. The French proposal made sound strategic sense but seemed oblivious to the inability of the French forces to stop the German advance. Given the condition of the French forces, it bordered on wishful thinking to suggest the Germans might not capture Paris before the counterattack could be organized.

Degoutte ordered the 2nd Division to occupy a line approximately 4 miles northwest of Château-Thierry, from the village of Bouresches, through Belleau, Torcy, and Bussiares. The village of Belleau controlled the crossroads leading to the Paris–Metz road. Between Belleau and Bouresches was the tangled forest known as the Bois de Belleau.

June 1, 1918

On June 1, the 9th Infantry Regiment deployed its 1st and 2nd Battalions on the right of the Allied line, extending the frontage of the French 43rd Division. The 3rd Battalion was kept back as a reserve. To the front of the 9th Regiment was a mixed unit of French. The French, unable to stop the Germans, were fighting a desperate rearguard action. During the late afternoon the 2/6th Marines arrived by truck, and at Harbord's request Bundy deployed the Marines on the left of the 9th Regiment, extending the American line to the west to Lucy-le-Bocage. As the 2/6th was deploying, Maj Edward Cole and the 6th Machine Gun Battalion arrived and two companies were sent forward to strengthen the line. Following the machine-gun units the 1/6th Marines and 3/6th Marines were directed by the commander of the 6th Regiment, Col Albertus Catlin, to the west. The 1/6th extended Catlin's line from Lucy to St Martin Wood and to Hill 142. Catlin placed the 3/6th in reserve in the woods north of Voie du Châtel.

During the night of June 1, Col Wendell Neville's 5th Marine Regiment settled down near Pyramid Farm, west of Lucy-le-Bocage. Later that night and during the early morning of June 2, the 23rd Infantry Regiment, commanded by Col Paul Malone, moved up to support the 9th Regiment. An officer of the 23rd Regiment described the French countryside:

The area we were in was untouched by war. It was farming country. There were fields with half grown wheat and occasionally fairly large stone farm buildings with large courtyards, though most farmworkers lived in the towns. There were small undulating hills and scattered hamlets. About every mile there would be a small patch of woods.

German bomber shot down near the 1st Division in early June, 1918.

Just after midnight, the 23rd Regiment, 1/5th, elements of the 5th Machine Gun Battalion, and a company of engineers moved to fill a gap on the left of the line. They were placed under the command of Gen Michel of the French 43rd Division and assigned to the VII Corps. The task force, under the command of Col Malone, marched 6 miles northwest of Lucy. Maj Julius Turrill's 1/5th Marines settled down near Premont. Elliot's 3/23rd extended Turrill's line further to the west and Waddill's 1/23rd moved north towards Brumetz. Elements of the 5th Machine Gun Battalion and engineers were distributed along the line.

June 2, 1918

The German attacks slowly pushed back the French defenders, driving some units back through the American lines. Brig Gen Harbord toured the positions held by the 23rd Regiment and Turrill's battalion and found little cause for optimism. Harbord ordered Col Neville to move his headquarters unit and Wise's 2/5th up to fill the gap between Turrill's battalion on the left and Maj Maurice Shearer's 1/6th on the right.

Around midday on June 2, the 2/5th established a defensive line from Veuilly Wood to the south of Les Mares Farm. Hill 165 rose one half-mile to their right front, while on the left Les Mares Farm was tucked into a fold in the fields. A unit of French Chasseurs was deployed around the farm and another group in the village of Champillon on the right. Directly behind them two batteries of French 75mm guns fired intermittently. Col Wise deployed his 51st Company on the right at Champillon, while the 55th Company occupied an area south of Les Mares Farm. The 18th and 43rd companies were extended to the left to Veuilly Wood. During the day, the Marines of the 18th Company reported the woods to their front, 700 yards distant, to be teeming with Germans.

Harbord informed Catlin that the Marines would have French artillery support. Sixty 75mm and 12 155mm guns were in position to assist the Americans, although they were very low on ammunition.

At about 1600hrs, Wise toured the Marine lines as German artillery fire began to increase. Wise telephoned regimental headquarters complaining that his flanks were in the air. Although the staff reassured him that support was nearby, Catlin ordered the 6th Marines to extend their lines to the west to contact Wise's right flank. In the late afternoon

Colonel Wise (right) commanded the 2/5th Marine Regiment. Wise's men successfully defended Les Mares Farm and fought in Belleau Wood.

the French batteries behind Wise's line withdrew without explanation, leaving the Americans even more isolated.

During the afternoon a German prisoner announced that a division would attack the American right flank. French Corps commander Gen Degoutte directed Maj Benjamin Berry's 3/5th into position behind the junction of the two brigades. Turrill's 1/5th was ordered to Pyramid Farm to act as Harbord's brigade reserve. Two machine-gun companies were also moved from the left to reinforce the 3rd Brigade.

As the afternoon slipped away, the 2nd Division's line began to stabilize. Despite their inability to stop the German advance, the French units in front of the American line delayed the Germans long enough for them to organize their defense. On the far left, Malone's three battalions were in position, although he still had no contact with French on his left. On the extreme right, Col LeRoy Upton's 9th Regiment had established a main line of defense. German artillery fire had increased throughout the day. The 1/6th, deployed in St Martin Wood opposite Belleau Wood, suffered a heavy barrage. At several points on the right of the 4th Brigade line the German advance punched through the French defenders, where heavy machine-gun fire from the Americans resulted in "dead Germans piled [on] the slopes."

In the center, the Marines tried to establish a continuous line. Despite their best efforts Wise's right flank failed to find Maj Berton Sibley's left near Hill 142. Both Wise and Shearer had been ordered to occupy Hill 142, the highest ground along their front. While Wise's right groped for Shearer's left, neither ended up moving up onto Hill 142.

During the course of the afternoon, French staff reported that Maj Thomas Holcomb's 2/6th had retreated. Catlin and Harbord were incredulous and frantically tried to sort out the truth. Holcomb later reassured his superiors that he was still in position, that the French had actually seen an engineering detachment moving to the rear to collect supplies. Despite the misunderstanding the incident highlighted the confused nature of the American deployment and the tendency of the French to believe the worst.

Early in the evening one final German effort pushed the French back all along the line. Just before midnight the Germans occupied the area south of Belleau–Torcy–Bussiares, advanced into the northern edge of Belleau Wood, and captured Hill 126. In response, Gen Degoutte began organizing a counterattack. Although he did not include the 2nd Division in his planning, he did postpone the handover of the sector to Bundy and the Americans.

Unaware that he was about to engage the Americans, Gen von Conta, commanding the German IV Reserve Corps, issued orders for a continuation of the offensive. The 197th Division was directed to capture the high ground at Marigny and Veuilly. The 237th Division was to focus on the area from Torcy to Lucy-le-Bocage, including Belleau Wood. The 10th Division would remain between Vaux and Bouresches, while the 231st and 36th divisions were to cross the Marne. The 5th Guards Division was kept in reserve to counterattack. With these orders the stage was set for the struggle over Belleau Wood.

June 3, 1918

The French counterattack threw the German advance off stride for a short time during the morning. Aimed primarily at the German 197th Division near Hill 142, the attack was disjointed and half-hearted, and collapsed by midday. Once the French attack had been blunted the Germans resumed the offensive.

The 237th Division moved into Belleau Wood, while on their right the 197th Division advanced cautiously south from Bussiares and Torcy. The unsuccessful counterattack seemed to have shaken the last bit of resolve from the French, and the German advance continued.

In the early morning, the 2nd Division's artillery was brought forward. The 12th and 15th regiments were armed with 75mm guns. The 12th was positioned to support the 4th Brigade while the 15th was to support the Marines. The 17th Regiment, with 155mm guns, was reinforced with five groups of French artillery and remained at the disposal of the divisional artillery commander.

In the afternoon, word was passed down from 2nd Division headquarters that the remaining French in front of the American positions would be retiring. Responsibility for this section of the line would be passed from the French 164th Division to the American 2nd Division.

Around 1600hrs a battalion of Senegalese began filtering back along the left flank of the 2/5th Battalion, many without weapons. The Chasseurs that had occupied Les Mares Farm also began to retire. As the French retreated one of their officers approached Capt Williams of the 51st Company and claimed to have written orders directing a general retreat. "Retreat, hell," retorted Williams. "We just got here."

Despite efforts by both commanding officers, the 2/5th was still unable to connect with Sibley's 3/6th. Contact between the left flank of the 2/5th and the 26th Regiment also proved elusive. In addition to his four companies in line, Wise had 12 machine guns of the 8th Machine Gun Company assigned to his left, while 12 guns from the other machine-gun companies protected his right. As the French withdrew Shearer directed two platoons from his reserve to extend to the left to make contact with Williams.

After the French had moved through the Marine lines and the German artillery picked up its pace, bracketing the Marines with the heaviest artillery fire they had yet experienced. The Marines watched with grim

determination as the lines of Germans from the 197th Division snaked out of the dark woods and began to cross the green wheatfields, moving towards Les Mares Farm. The farm was approximately 35 miles from Paris and would represent the high water mark of the German offensive.

The Germans were formed into extended lines, with six paces between each man, four or five lines 25 yards apart, bayonets fixed. Col Wise was worried that their lines overlapped the flanks of his battalion. Catlin and his brigade staff watched from their headquarters at La Voie du Châtel.

The Marines allowed the Germans to close to within 300 yards before opening up with aimed rifle fire and machine guns. The Germans seemed momentarily stunned at the fury and accuracy of the American fire, which eviscerated their forward lines. Several times over the next hour the Germans organized an advance, only to be driven to ground by Marine rifle fire. American artillery also joined the attack. The German advance had not extended beyond the flanks of the 2/5th as Wise had feared, but had been funneled between two wooded areas, along the road leading directly to Les Mares Farm.

The Germans retired into the protection of the woods and engaged in a desultory exchange of machine-gun fire. Von Conta's right wing had fallen well short of its objectives and suffered 800 casualties in their attacks. Ludendorff had emphasized that Operation *Blücher* was to be a limited offensive, but as the French resistance continued to crumple the German advance rolled on. Ludendorff directed that defensive formations must be maintained and advised his commanders to recognize "the moment the attack must be stopped and defense resumed. This must be felt by the systematic hardening of the enemy's resistance."

Von Conta now seemed to recognize that his men had experienced the "systematic hardening," although he was at a loss to explain why here and why now. His orders for June 4 directed his divisional commanders to suspend the offensive. The order stated that:

> *Corps Conta … is compelled to temporarily assume the defensive, after positions most suitable for this purpose are captured. The offensive spirit must be maintained even though a temporary lull in the attack seems to exist. In the general purpose of the operations, no halt or lull exists. We are the victors and will remain on the offensive. The enemy is defeated and the High Command will utilize this great success to the fullest extent.*

4th Brigade orders for June 4 were much simpler. Both Neville and Catlin were told that:

General Harbord directs that the necessary steps be taken to hold our positions at all costs.

During the early evening, the 30th Regiment of the 3rd Division crossed the Marne and relieved a battalion of the 9th Regiment near Mont de Bonneil.

Interlude, June 4, 1918

After the repulse at Les Mares Farm, the Germans and Americans settled down to an uneasy period of waiting. The Americans had struck a blow that was not fatal and did not inflict any long-lasting damage, but the swiftness and strength of the strike had surprised the Germans.

The American line was connected with the French 167th Division on the left, and on the right with the French 39th Division. The 39th Division then connected to their right with the American 3rd Division in Château-Thierry. Facing the American 2nd Division were elements of the German IV Reserve Corps.

The general disposition of the 2nd Division had the 23rd Regiment holding the left of the line. Berry's 3/5th was deployed as the brigade reserve in wooded areas southwest of Marigny. The 1/5th and 2/5th held the forward positions, supplemented by elements of the regimental headquarters company. The 6th Marines were clustered around Pyramid Farm, facing Bouresches and Belleau Wood on their left. Brigade headquarters was moved to La Loge. Late in the day Wise's 2/5th Marines were withdrawn and placed in reserve to support the 1/5th and 3/5th.

Despite all attempts over the past several days, the junction of the 5th and 6th Marines still posed a problem. Maj Sibley had discovered that the retreating French had uncovered a half-mile gap, through which passed the main road from Torcy and Lucy. Presumably the German advance, when it resumed, would follow this road to the south.

The right of the American line was held by the 9th Regiment. On June 4, the French 167th Division moved up to relieve the 26th Regiment on the far left. The 26th Regiment moved to join the 9th Regiment on the right. The 26th occupied the area held by 2/6th forming a link between the 6th Marine Regiment and the 9th Regiment.

While some supplies, particularly ammunition, were brought forward, the rolling kitchens that the infantry relied upon for hot meals were only now settling down in secure areas. The men of the 2nd Division instead prepared "trench donuts" made by frying bread in bacon grease and applying liberal amounts of sugar. Water was a more immediate problem. The closest supply was a mile away. Runners were required to carry up to 20 canteens two or three times a day.

Although the main German offensive had been suspended, they continued their general bombardment of the Marine lines and launched small probing attacks, which were driven off. By this time the American troops had become well acquainted with the variety of German artillery. The large "sea bags" 210mm trench mortars, slow but powerful, and the 150mm "Jack Johnsons" with their large plumes of

American machine-gun crew dug in to stop German advance.

black smoke, contrasted with the 88mm "quick dicks" and 77mm "whiz bang" rounds which gave little warning.

While their artillery pummeled the American lines, the German infantry was occupying Belleau Wood. The 461st Regiment deployed in Belleau Wood and set up defensive lines. They occupied the southern and western face of the wood and established contact with elements of the 10th Division to the east at Bouresches.

During the afternoon, small units of the Saxon 26th Jäger Regiment began infiltrating from the surrounding woods into the wheat fields bordering Les Mares Farm. The Marines dispatched a small patrol to investigate. The patrol found 30 Germans with two machine guns attempting to dig in. After a furious firefight the Germans were driven off and the guns captured. It was on June 4 that the Germans recovered the body of a dead American and identified him as a Marine.

During the afternoon of June 4, 1918, Gen Pershing visited Harbord and Bundy and congratulated the 2nd Division and Marine Brigade on their efforts.

June 5, 1918
Both sides spent June 5 in an uneasy standoff. Despite their success in stopping the German advance, the Americans were suffering from a serious lack of operational intelligence. The French had provided 19th-century elementary maps of the battlefield and no aerial reconnaissance. The Marines lacked detailed knowledge of the terrain and troop strength of the German units. Since arriving at the front the Americans had been too focused on stabilizing their lines to spend time gathering information.

On June 4, Harbord ordered regimental commanders to send out small patrols to locate the enemy positions. The American patrols gathered meager information about the enemy dispositions. They did note activity in Belleau Wood, but this intelligence was at odds with other information from the French, who reported that the Germans occupied only the northeast section of the wood. The French report described the situation in Belleau Wood as they were retiring on June 3, rather than any recent assessment.

Gen Degoutte was eager to shift the initiative and go on the offensive. At 1500hrs on June 5, Degoutte issued orders for an attack on June 6, 1918. The French 167th Division was directed to jump off at 1545hrs and capture the high ground south of Clignon Creek. Coupled with this advance, the left of the 2nd Division, the 5th Marines, would also advance. Once this attack was completed the remainder of the 2nd Division was ordered to capture Belleau Wood and occupy the high ground overlooking Belleau and Torcy.

Degoutte's desire to go over to the attack, coupled with Bundy and Harbord's need to prove that the 2nd Division was up to the task, blinded the High Command to the need to gather more intelligence about enemy strength and their dispositions. Although Col Brown had dissuaded Degoutte from committing units of the 2nd Division piecemeal on June 1, and the example of Degoutte's failed counter-attack of June 3 should have been fresh on their minds, Degoutte was again intent on committing the 2nd Division without regard for proper planning, and this time Brown and Bundy willingly acceded.

Harbord and Divisional Chief of Staff Col Brown immediately began preparations for the next days' attacks. Turrill's 1/5th would attack in conjunction with the French 167th Division. Turrill's objective would be Hill 142, which had been occupied by the Germans after Wise and Sibley's failure to link up. Brown stressed that the Americans should utilize infiltration tactics rather than advance by wave, and closely coordinate their advance with artillery. Despite that advice Harbord limited the duration of the preparatory artillery barrage, not wanting to alert the enemy to the Marine attack. American artillery would provide erratic fire throughout the night and a short barrage as the Marines jumped off. Little tactical planning was done for the afternoon attack.

For the afternoon attack Harbord tapped Berry's 3/5th. At 1700hrs Berry was to move due east into the northern portion of Belleau Wood. On Berry's right, Sibley's 3/6th was to capture the southern section of the wood and then move on to Bouresches. Maj Holcomb's 2/6th was ordered to protect Sibley's right flank and maintain contact with the left flank of the 23rd Regiment. With no intelligence to the contrary Harbord believed the wood to be lightly held and ordered a limited artillery barrage to support the Marines.

Although the 2nd Division had acquitted itself well in stopping the German advance, those static defensive operations required far less tactical finesse than did the initiation of successful attacks. The daunting task facing the 4th Brigade was further complicated when Harbord ordered several redeployments after dark on June 5. Wise's 2/5th was to be relieved by the French 167th Division, while Berry's 3/5th was to relieve Shearer's 1/6th and elements of the 23rd Regiment were to relieve Holcomb's 2/6th. Berry's battalion would occupy a line that ran southeast from just east of Hill 142 to just north of Lucy-le-Bocage, facing the western face of Belleau Wood. Turrill's 1/5th was to relieve the three companies of Sibley's 3/6th, which was to regroup south of Belleau Wood for the afternoon attack. While these movements would reduce the area for which the 4th Brigade was responsible, the shifting of so many units, already worn out, over unfamiliar ground, with inadequate maps, on the eve of a major offensive, at night, and under constant German artillery fire could only result in confusion.

At 2100hrs Frank Evans, adjutant of the 6th Marines, issued a note to Sibley advising him that he and his men would be relieved by Turrill's 1/5th in preparation for their attack at 0345hrs. It would be several hours before Turrill received his orders.

At 2245hrs Field Order Number One was issued, directing Turrill's 1/5th, supported by the 8th and 23rd Machine Gun companies and Company D of the 2nd Engineers, to attack "between the brook of Champillon, inclusive, Hill 142 and the brook which flows from one kilometer northeast of Champillon, inclusive." Berry's 3/5th would cover Turrill's right flank and both battalions were ordered to consolidate their positions on the far side of Hill 142 and expect a counterattack.

5th Marine commander, Col Neville, passed on the order at 0035hrs, correcting the directive to accurately characterize the "brooks" as ravines. Turrill received the order just as he was bringing 67th and 49th companies into line. His remaining companies and the 8th Machine Gun Company were still waiting at Les Mares Farm to be relieved by the French. He knew nothing of the whereabouts of the 23rd Machine Gun Company or the engineers, although he did have ten machine guns from the 15th Machine Gun Company available to support his attack.

Lt Col Feland, Neville's assistant, joined Turrill as Crowther and Hamilton were briefed on the attack. Hill 142 was actually a finger of high ground, sloping north, down from Hill 176 towards Torcy. It was covered by alternating patches of wheatfield and woods. The orders were simple enough. Crowther would direct his company north, resting his flank on the ravine to his left. Hamilton would also move north, capturing the crest of the hill and securing the eastern slope. Hamilton was to expect support on the right from Berry's 3/5th.

Hill 142 was strongly held by the enemy. The hill was the boundary between the 237th and 197th divisions. The 460th Regiment of the 237th Division deployed a battalion on the eastern slope, while a battalion of the 273rd Regiment, 197th Division defended the western sector. Like their American counterparts, confusion over the boundary between the defending units limited effective coordination. Regardless, the Germans had sprinkled machine-gun emplacements throughout the wooded areas and were alert to the American attack after a night under intermittent artillery fire.

The German 28th Division issued orders on June 5 to advance the next day between Bouresches and Hill 204 and cut the Paris–Metz road and take the high ground around Aulnois Bontemps Farm. The attack of the 4th Brigade would render those orders obsolete.

HILL 142

As morning came, the American artillery began their short barrage right on schedule. The machine guns of the 15th Company added their weight to the pre-assault barrage. Despite the directive of Col Brown to use infiltration tactics, the Marines were inexplicably deployed to advance in the standard French line of sections formation. In the confusion in passing along orders from Brown and Harbord to their subordinate commanders the tactical directive was lost or overlooked, leaving the leaders with an alternative directive from Bundy, issued some weeks earlier, in which he encouraged his officers to use the more compact wave formation which he believed would "ensure the highest degree of control by subordinate commanders."

American field kitchen deployed to serve men of the 4th Brigade.

Turrill was still missing two of his companies, and neither Crowther nor Hamilton had been able to establish contact with the units assigned to protect their flanks. At 0345hrs, as the barrage began to march across Hill 142, the company commanders blew their whistles and platoon commanders pointed towards the hidden enemy. Over the eastern horizon the sun began to rise, turning the sky red, and heralding what would be the bloodiest day in Marine Corps history.

The Marines moving out across the green wheatfields had shed their backpacks, carrying only their weapons, bandoliers of extra ammunition, a few grenades, and gas masks. The Marines had barely covered 50 yards when the Germans began firing. Harbord's decision to minimize artillery preparation allowed the Germans to react quickly to the Marine advance. Instinctively, both companies fell to the ground to escape the Maxim fire. German snipers in the trees added to the carnage.

Turrill, watching his men being cut to ribbons, frantically requested the machine guns supporting the attack to turn their fire into the woods to their front. Realizing that to stay in the wheatfield meant certain death, Capt George Hamilton jumped to his feet and cajoled a dozen or more men to rise and follow him in a mad rush towards the woods. Hamilton later wrote in a letter:

Drawing of ruined church in Lucy-le-Bocage. Lucy was used by the Marines as a staging area for their attacks on Belleau Wood throughout June, 1918.

From here on I don't remember clearly what happened. I have a vague recollection of urging the whole line on … faster perhaps, than they should have gone, of grouping prisoners and sending them to the rear under one man instead of several, of snatching an Iron Cross off the first officer I got, of shooting wildly at several rapidly retreating Boche. I carried a rifle on the whole trip and used it to good

55

German artillery deployed in the French countryside to support the defense of Belleau Wood. German artillery would take their toll on the Marines throughout the struggle for Belleau Wood.

advantage. Farther on we came to an open field, a wheatfield full of red poppies, and here we caught hell. Again it was a case of rushing across the open and getting into the woods. Afterwards we found out why it was they made it so hot for us. Three machine-gun companies were holding down these woods…

Hamilton, looking for his objective, an unimproved road just beyond Hill 142, led his men over the nose of the hill and down into another field beyond. One of Hamilton's platoons peeled off to secure Hill 142. Hamilton and a small group advanced almost 600 yards beyond Hill 142 to a stone bridge before Hamilton realized he had gone too far. The group was forced to crawl along a shallow drainage ditch. While Hamilton and his companions returned to Hill 142, another small group of three Marines advanced towards the village of Torcy. Sending one Marine back for reinforcements, the other two established themselves in a house where they tried in vain to hold off a battalion of Germans. They were never seen alive again.

The 67th Company was also pinned down in the wheatfields, and Capt Crowther was killed trying to direct his men forward. Corporal Geer, later awarded the Navy Cross for his actions, took Crowther's place and led the Marines forward to rush the enemy guns and secure their portion of Hill 142.

At approximately 0630hrs, Capt Hamilton reorganized his small force, composed of the survivors of his company and the now leaderless 67th Company, on the north slope of Hill 142. The Marines quickly organized a ragged defensive line. Hamilton found that both his flanks were open and conformed his line to the curvature of Hill 142.

The German counterattack was not long in coming. Led by the 7th Saxon Jägers, groups of Germans using infiltration tactics popped up among the defenders. The Marines responded with bayonet charges and desperate hand-to-hand struggles erupted along the entire line. As the battle hung in the balance, Gunnery Sergeant Charles Hoffman and Capt Hamilton noted a group of Germans dragging five machine guns through the brush. Before Hamilton could respond he was slightly wounded by an exploding grenade. Hoffman charged alone down the

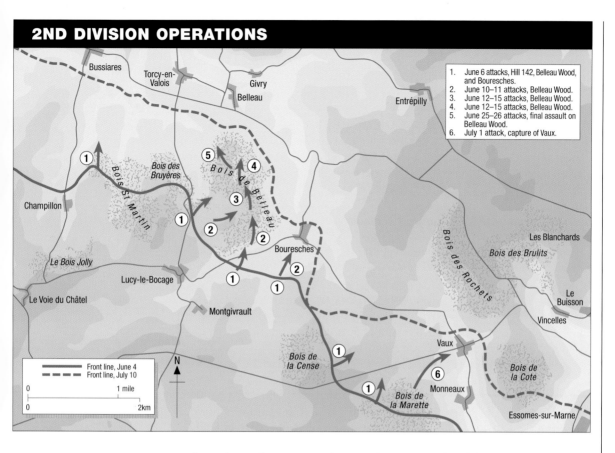

Bussiares
Torcy-en-Valois
Givry
Belleau
Entrépilly

1. June 6 attacks, Hill 142, Belleau Wood, and Bouresches.
2. June 10–11 attacks, Belleau Wood.
3. June 12–15 attacks, Belleau Wood.
4. June 12–15 attacks, Belleau Wood.
5. June 25–26 attacks, final assault on Belleau Wood.
6. July 1 attack, capture of Vaux.

Bois des Bruyères
Bois de Belleau
Bois St Martin
Champillon
Le Bois Jolly
Lucy-le-Bocage
Le Voie du Châtel
Montgivrault
Bouresches
Bois des Rochets
Les Blanchards
Bois des Brulits
Le Buisson
Vincelles
Bois de la Cense
Vaux
Monneaux
Bois de la Cote
Bois de la Marette
Essomes-sur-Marne

Front line, June 4
Front line, July 10

0   1 mile
0   2km

N

slope into the enemy, bayoneting two. Joined by several Marines, Hoffman was badly wounded but the Germans were killed or captured. For his action, Hoffman became the first member of the 2nd Division to win the Congressional Medal of Honor.

Guns from the 8th Machine Gun Company finally arrived and deployed along the eastern slope. Turrill also hurried forward the 17th Company, 66th Company, and elements of the 2nd Engineers to reinforce Hamilton's men. By 0900hrs reports of prisoners and wounded Marines had begun to filter back to Neville's command post. Hamilton reported that he needed both ammunition and stretchers and, while he held the hill, all his officers were dead or wounded. Lt Col Feland rushed to the front with Turrill. Feland ordered the 51st Company, 2/5th up to protect the left flank and the 45th Company, 3/5th to extend the right flank.

The immediate aftermath of the struggle for Hill 142 established a pattern that was to plague the 4th Brigade throughout the next several weeks. Overly optimistic reports, devoid in many cases of any real sense of the reality of the situation, were issued by battalion and regimental commanders. Reported numbers of prisoners taken ranged from 50 to 300, when the final accounting showed only 15.

Reports from the wounded returning from the battle also added to the confusion. At Wise's 2/5th battalion headquarters at La Voie du Châtel the walking wounded and those carried on stretchers were gathered in the courtyard. The Marines were tired and despondent, reporting that the attack had failed and the battalion been decimated. A shell-shocked captain of engineers claimed that the Marines had been cut to ribbons. When Wise threatened to shoot him he burst into tears and continued his way to the rear. These erroneous reports were further aggravated by the reluctance of senior commanders, such as Harbord and Neville, to actually visit the front line.

What was becoming clear to Harbord and Neville was the cost of the victory. Hamilton reported 90 percent of the officers from the two assault companies were down and total strength reduced by 50 percent. Turrill reported at noon that total casualties were about 335 men.

On the left of the Americans, the French 167th Division moved off smartly at 0345hrs, preceded by a brief but violent artillery barrage. Although the French infantry pushed quickly towards Bussiares, over-running several German positions, their artillery failed to adjust its fire and shells began to fall among the infantry. Fired on from the front and rear, with casualties mounting, the attack fell apart. Shaken and confused, the French infantry retired to their starting point. While their officers were able to reorganize another attack later on the afternoon of June 6, the unenthusiastic assault failed to gain any ground. This seesaw movement by the French resulted in Turrill's left flank hanging in the air throughout the morning until Capt Lloyd Williams' 51st Company was ordered to move forward. Although not engaged in the initial assault, Williams would suffer 50 casualties.

On the right, 3/5th struggled to keep contact with Turrill's battalion. Capt Peter Conachy's 45th Company was assigned the task of connecting to Hamilton's 49th Company. At 0600hrs Conachy's leftmost platoon reported that it was one half-mile from Hill 142 and encountering large groups of Germans. Turrill reported that he heard firing from his right but there was still no sign of men from Conachy's company. By noon Conachy had reported over 70 casualties. Both commanders noted the same patch of woods, not shown on their maps, had frustrated their attempts to secure contact. Those woods were occupied by two companies of German infantry.

Throughout the remainder of June 6 the survivors of Turrill's 1/5th tightened their grip on Hill 142. Turrill sent Neville several requests for ammunition. At 1240hrs, Turrill sent a terse assessment to Neville, suggesting that if Berry's troops did not show up on his right he might be forced to fall back. At 1310hrs Turrill notified Neville that the French had finally shown up on his left.

While Turrill was justifiably concerned about the losses sustained during his morning attack, the situation of the Germans was no better. The American thrust had badly mauled the 197th Division, which reported over 2,000 casualties between June 4 and 6, with the majority incurred on the last day. The 273rd Regiment reported over 400 casualties on the morning of June 6. Responding to a request for reinforcements from the 197th Division, two battalions of the 5th Prussian Guards Division were deployed behind the 273rd Regiment.

As the battle for Hill 142 raged, Lt Cooke of the 18th Company, 2/5th, greeted 2nd Lt Zischke, carrying an armload of Paris newspapers. The headlines announced that the Marines had saved Paris. American war correspondent Floyd Gibbons had fought a running battle with American military censors who refused to allow reporters to name individual units. As the 2nd Division became engaged in battle, Gibbons and others argued that they should be able to differentiate between the regular Army and

American machine-gun batteries like these were deployed to secure Hill 142 after its capture early on June 6, 1918.

Marines. The censors finally consented to allow Gibbons to refer to the Marines in his stories describing the stopping of the German offensive. Given that there were only two units of Marines, both in the 2nd Division, it was not difficult to determine which units were engaged in battle. The release of the news highlighting the actions of the Marines electrified the American public. On June 6, the *Chicago Tribune* boasted:

US MARINES SMASH HUNS GAIN GLORY IN BRISK FIGHT ON THE MARNE CAPTURE MACHINE GUNS, KILL BOCHES, TAKE PRISONERS

ATTACK ON BELLEAU WOOD

As Degoutte, Bundy, and Harbord assessed the situation around noon, the first phase of the planned offensive had gone reasonably well. While the French 167th Division had not kept pace with Turrill's advance, Degoutte simply ordered them forward again. Reports from Hill 142 indicated it had been captured, although the American position was still tenuous and casualties high. Securing Hill 142 had required the deployment of one company of Wise's 2/5th and Berry's 3/5th, removing what were already limited resources from the attack on Belleau Wood. In setting in motion the assault on Belleau Wood, Bundy and Harbord were operating, once again, from a complete lack of intelligence concerning the size or disposition of the enemy. Several days prior to the attack an American intelligence officer had attempted to locate the Germans and had identified enemy activity on the western edge of Belleau Wood. Despite those reports, Harbord and Bundy based their plans on the faulty French intelligence which suggested only the northeast corner of the wood was held in strength by the Germans.

At the same time as orders were being issued for the attack, Maj Bischoff, a veteran of bush fighting in East Africa, was supervising the organization of the defenses in Belleau Wood. Bischoff commanded the 461st Regiment, with a strength of 1,169 men, of the 237th Division.

Bischoff's men had worked quickly to take advantage of the broken terrain within the wood, rock outcroppings surrounded by dense undergrowth, to deploy their machine guns. Rather than one line of trenches there were three. The southernmost trench line was set back from the edge of the wood and protected a small plateau. Among the boulders in the center of this raised area, Bischoff positioned 15 machine guns in mutually supporting locations. Across the narrow neck of the wood a second trench line was constructed. Barbed wire was strung across the approaches to the second line of defense. Trench mortars were also deployed in this second line. The strongest defenses were constructed across the northern section of the wood. This line of trenches featured more machine guns and trench mortars, protected by barbed wire. In all, Bischoff crowded 200 machine guns into Belleau Wood.

At 1405hrs Harbord issued Field Order Number Two, which set out the details for the attack on Belleau Wood and the village of Bouresches. Col Catlin of the 6th Regiment would command the attack. On the left, Berry's 3/5th, now under Catlin's command, would move down the hill, across the open field, and into the western section of Belleau Wood.

Consistent with the flawed intelligence, Harbord ordered a limited artillery barrage to rake the northern and eastern slopes of the wood coupled with interdicting fire to the north and east. The Marines stepping off at 1700hrs would face an enemy undisturbed by artillery.

To the east of the wood, the 461st Regiment tied into the 398th Regiment, 10th Division. The 398th Regiment held a line through the villages of Bouresches and Vaux. In Bouresches, a reinforced company dug in around the railroad station and in ruined houses.

Harbord's plan proposed that Berry's 3/5th, minus Conachy's company, which had been moved up to support Turrill on Hill 142, attack the western face of the wood. Once Berry had secured the wood his battalion was to move north, capturing Hill 133. To Berry's right, Maj Sibley's 3/6th was ordered to attack the southwest edge of the wood and move through the wood to capture Bouresches. Maj Holcomb's 2/6th, on Sibley's right, was to pivot its left in alignment with Sibley's advance. Col Catlin would be in overall command, responsible for his 6th Regiment and Berry's 3/5th. Catlin received the orders at 1545hrs, which set the jump-off time for 1700hrs. Catlin briefed Holcomb and Sibley in the gulley south of Belleau Wood. Catlin had no direct communications with Berry, and orders to attack reached the 3/5th at 1645hrs.

Berry realized that he had no chance to coordinate the movements of his companies, with only a few minutes until the attack was scheduled to begin. To make matters worse, Berry disregarded the directive to leave Conachy's 45th Company behind to assist Turrill. While Conachy was at Turrill's headquarters coordinating his movements, Berry scooped up the 45th Company and directed them into the assault. Each company of the 3/5th was ordered to leave a single platoon in reserve as the battalion crossed 400 yards of open ground. From left to right all four companies would advance abreast.

Catlin briefed Holcomb and Sibley, using a map to outline their intended movements, while Sibley's men filed into the ravine south of the wood. Catlin continued to be concerned about Berry's advance and their lack of direct communications. He decided to monitor Berry's attack from a vantage point west of the wood. As Sibley's men were nervously waiting to attack, Catlin passed nearby and was asked to give the men some words of encouragement. He said simply, "Give 'em Hell boys." Catlin later wrote:

> *The men seemed cool, in good spirits and ready for the word to start. They were talking quietly among themselves. I spoke to several as I passed... On my left I passed some of Berry's men, the right end of his battalion. They too seemed to be ready and waiting for the leash to be slipped...*

Catlin and his French liaison Capt Laspierre moved to a small rise 300 yards from Belleau Wood, protected by a low hedge, to watch the attack.

Sibley organized his attack with Capt Dwight Smith's 82nd and Capt Alfred Noble's 83rd companies directed to move left of the ravine into the southwest portion of Belleau Wood and then continue through the southern section and support the capture of Bouresches. Capt Mark Smith's 84th and Capt Tom McEvoy's 97th were to advance towards Bouresches. Sibley ordered his men to advance in line of sections consistent with their French training. Sibley's tactical directive was repeated by Berry and Holcomb. Rather than utilize infiltration tactics which emphasized fire and maneuver, the Marines would leave the shelter of the woods, with each battalion formed with their companies deploying two platoons in front and two behind, creating neat lines. This formation put a premium on command and control. It also provided the German machine guns and artillery with a perfect target.

After receiving his briefing from Catlin, Maj Holcomb sent an urgent message to Capt Donald Duncan's 96th Company, on his far right, which was deployed behind Malone's 23rd Regiment. Duncan received the message with less than 30 minutes until the attack. He quickly assembled his men and started them forward, over 1,000 yards, to their departure line.

Orders were also sent to Wise, directing him to move the 2/5th into Berry's vacated positions once the attack began. Wise marched his men into the southern portion of the wooded area held by Berry. Berry met briefly with Wise and a witness reported that both men looked worried.

Miscommunication and confusion increased as the orders from Harbord moved down the line. 3rd Brigade commander Brig Gen Lewis issued his own field order at 1515hrs, ordering Malone's 23rd Regiment to coordinate its leftmost battalion with the movements of the Marines. Concerned that the movement of Holcomb's 2/6th toward Bouresches would create a re-entrant angle, he directed both Maj Waddill's 1/23rd and Maj Charles Elliot's 3/23rd to advance several hundred yards towards Hill 192. Lewis briefed Elliot at 1615hrs and finally reached Waddill at 1655hrs. At the same time, Lewis received a notice that at 2130hrs the French 10th Colonial Regiment would attack Hill 204 on his right. Lewis was directed to ensure that Upton's 9th Regiment would maintain liaison with the French.

The limited artillery barrage began at 1630hrs. Machine guns from the 77th and 81st companies added firepower but the thick woods concealing the enemy limited their effectiveness. While everyone but Harbord suspected Belleau Wood was strongly held, Harbord's subsequent explanation that he didn't want to alert the Germans to the impending attack with a proper artillery barrage is even more troubling. After the morning's attack on Hill 142, the Germans would have been foolish to

American infantry in defensive positions. The Marines at Les Mares Farm deployed in a similar fashion, digging shallow foxholes.

ignore the growing pressure on Belleau Wood. Rather, German observation balloons had noted the movements of the Marines throughout the day and German artillery had been directed at the areas of concentration. Berry's and Wise's men suffered from increasing German artillery fire as time for the jump off approached. Inside the wood the 461st Regiment was reinforced with two additional companies.

Berry's 3/5th stepped out at 1700hrs, moving down a sloping wheatfield towards Belleau Wood. While the 45th Company advanced as ordered, platoons from the 16th Company were only given orders to advance as the American barrage died down. As one lieutenant wrote:

> This was the first information we had received regarding an attack and did not know one had been planned. No objective was given as to where to stop and no maps had been distributed; the only thing we were sure of was the direction and we knew that.

Wave upon wave of Marines walked out of the shadows of the cool woods into hell.

The shortcomings of the American tactical formations were attested to after the battle by the German LtCol Ernst Otto. Otto wrote:

> the attack of the 3rd Battalion, 5th Marines and the 2nd and 3rd Battalions … was directed chiefly against the left wing of the 398th Regiment, particularly the 1st Battalion and the right wing of the 47th Regiment, 1st Battalion. The Americans were obliged to come down from the heights they were occupying before the eyes of the Germans. They did this in thick lines of skirmishers, supported by columns following immediately behind. The Germans could not have desired better targets; such a spectacle was entirely unfamiliar to them. German troops would have advanced in thin lines of skirmishers following one another in waves, or in small separate units of shock troops, moving forward in rows with their light machine guns, utilizing whatever shelter was offered by the terrain until they were in a position to open fire.

The American formation pleased Catlin, who later wrote:

> I say they went in as if on parade, and that is literally true. There was no yell and wild rush, but a deliberate forward march, with lines at dress right. They walked at regulation pace, because a man is little use in a hand-to-hand bayonet struggle after a hundred-yard dash.

Journalist Floyd Gibbons, himself grievously wounded when accompanying the advance of Berry's troops, described the American tactics somewhat differently. He wrote:

> *...our men advanced in open order, ten and twelve feet between men. Sometimes a squad would run forward fifty feet and drop. And as its members flattened on the ground for safety another squad would rise from the ground and make another rush.*

In either case the results were catastrophic. The German machine guns filled the air with lead, tearing up the parade-ground formation, littering wheatfields with dead and dying Americans and driving those unwounded into cover. In the face of the withering fire, Berry's men dropped into the wheat, gaining little ground. The 47th Company made slightly more progress, struggling into the southwest corner of Belleau Wood. Just after 1800hrs Berry sent a message back to Catlin informing him that what was left of the battalion had advanced into the wood but he was uncertain if they would survive. Berry moved into the field trying to gather more information and was seriously wounded.

To Berry's right, Sibley's 3/6th moved out, straddling the Lucy–Bouresches road towards the southern edge of the wood, with two companies on the north and two on the south side of the ravine. Heavy machine-gun fire burst from the wood, pinning down the 82nd Company. The 83rd Company moved through the stalled company and fought their way into the wood, followed by the 82nd. They advanced several hundred yards, capturing a number of machine guns and several *minenwerfers* (mortars). Once inside the wood the Marines broke into small groups fighting intense, deadly battles with German machine guns, well hidden and supported by infantry. Grenades and bayonets were the weapons of choice in what one officer later described as "an exaggerated riot." The companies lost contact with each other in the dense undergrowth and the failing light. Elements of the 23rd Machine Gun Company, which had supported the initial attack, joined the infantry as daylight slipped away.

The other two companies of the 3/6th, the 84th and 97th, skirted the edge of the wood and advanced into the wheatfields where they were pinned down by machine-gun fire. Although protected by a small rise of fire from Bouresches, the Marines were surprised at the fire coming from their left flank and rear, areas of the wood they had just passed through. The Americans charged back into the wood and carved out a small defensive position. Sibley ordered them to hold where they were and informed Harbord that his advance had stalled short of their objective.

As he watched Berry and Sibley attack the wood, Col Catlin was wounded in the chest by a sniper. Lt Col Lee took command of the 6th Marines. Lee tried to sort out the confused situation, reporting to Harbord that Sibley's battalion had been roughly handled. Apparently ignorant of the grievous losses and the wounding of Berry, Harbord chastised Lee for not directing Berry's and Sibley's battalions to continue their assault. Harbord also continued to send orders to Catlin.

On Sibley's right, Holcomb's 2/6th was ordered to support the assault on Bouresches. The 79th Company, led by Capt Randolf Zane, provided a loose connection with Sibley's command. Zane's men were decimated by German machine-gun and artillery fire. With the failure of Sibley's advance the 96th Company was directed to capture Bouresches, supported by several platoons of the 79th Company. Machine-gun support was provided by a composite force made up from the 81st, 77th, and 73rd companies.

The 96th Company, led by Capt Donald Duncan, deployed into skirmish lines and moved along the La Cense ravine, taking what cover they could from Triangle Wood. Duncan directed one platoon, commanded by Lt Clifton Cates, to move along the western edge of Belleau Wood, while the other three advanced along the eastern side through the open fields. The 2nd, 3rd, and 4th platoons broke out of the woods at a trot, firing as they advanced. They had to cross 600 yards of open fields. Although Duncan was killed early in the advance and scores more were killed and wounded, the Marines got within 200 yards of Bouresches before the German fire drove the 2nd Platoon to ground and forced the others to take refuge in a ravine. Cates' platoon rushed forward, entered Bouresches, and destroyed the machine guns delaying the advance, allowing the remainder of the company to move forward. Cates directed his small force, just over 30 men, to set up defensive positions to block the expected German counterattack. While making his way towards the railroad station, still in German hands, Cates' small group suffered further casualties from machine-gun fire. After destroying the machine-gun nests Cates and his force of 21 men nervously settled down to defend the town. As German shelling subsided, elements of Zane's 79th Company which had sought shelter in Belleau Wood with the 84th Company moved back into the open field and rejoined their comrades, and together they found their way into Bouresches to bolster the defense.

During the attack, the remainder of the 2/6th suffered through heavy German artillery fire, including gas, limiting their ability to provide any support to the defense of Bouresches. To their right, Col Malone watched the Marine advance and notified Maj Waddill 1/23rd and Maj Charles Elliot 3/23rd to be ready to move forward in coordination with the Marines. Waddill reported that the Marine company on his left had no orders to advance. While Malone left to confer with 3rd Brigade commander Brig Gen Lewis, Elliot made plans to advance. At 1800hrs he directed two companies forward. Waddill, noting the appearance of Elliot's men far advanced on his right, also ordered his battalion forward at 1900hrs.

Elliot's companies advanced towards the Germans dug in behind the railroad bed, east of Bouresches. The Germans had an unobstructed view of the American advance and responded with heavy machine-gun fire and artillery barrages. By 2100hrs, Elliot reported heavy casualties and asked for assistance. At 2130hrs, Waddill's battalion occupied their objective. Confused messages continued to be received by Malone throughout the evening, including an erroneous report that Elliot's line had been broken. At 2255hrs Malone notified Elliot that he was to retire to his starting line before dawn. A German counterattack at 0100hrs hastened his retirement along with Waddill's battalion.

On the far right, Upton's regiment advanced as planned but ran into a German artillery barrage. Upton's men were then subjected to an American counterbarrage that fell in their lines adding to the casualties.

Despite the confusion, the 9th Regiment reached their objective line, made contact with the French on their right, and dug in.

The German artillery also blanketed the portion of Belleau Wood held by Sibley's two companies with gas. Sibley's men were joined by two companies of the 2nd Engineers after nightfall. At 2230hrs Harbord, now well aware of the tenuous nature of the positions held by his troops, ordered Sibley to dig in and try to establish contact with elements of Berry's 3/5th on his left. Lt Col Lee, who had replaced Catlin as commander of the 6th Marines, sent a note to Harbord at 2330hrs describing the positions of Berry's 20th and 47th Companies which had penetrated Belleau Wood, and asking for grenades and 37mm guns.

Marine strength in Bouresches continued to grow, as groups of men from Holcomb's 2/6th straggled into the town. Holcomb established his headquarters in a ravine 800 yards southwest of the town. Just before midnight Holcomb, unsure of the location of his men, sent a message to regimental headquarters, suggesting that Zane's company was unable to advance and requesting that Maj Robert Messersmith's 78th Company be directed to Bouresches. At the same time the 78th Company was the target of a gas attack, eliminating it from any support role.

Turrill, joined by Lt Col Logan Feland, Neville's second in command, spent the remainder of June 6 consolidating their hold on Hill 142 and trying to establish contact with either Berry on their right or the French on their left. Feland sent Harbord several messages asking for ammunition and medical assistance. Still apparently ignorant of the desperate condition of Turrill's command, Harbord considered ordering a resumption of the offensive to conform to the original plan. He approved a request by Feland for an artillery barrage at 2030hrs. Lack of adequate information continued to hobble Harbord. Maj Cole, 6th Machine Gun Battalion, reported that

How Twenty Marines Took Bouresches by Frank Schoonover, *Ladies Home Journal*, 1918. On June 6, 1918, American Marines advanced through green wheatfields, strewn with red poppies, to capture the village of Bouresches. Despite heavy losses a small group of Marines made their way into Bouresches and drove the German defenders out. (Courtesy of Delaware National Guard)

Lee's men had reached the northern portion of Belleau Wood, when the reality was that they were strung out along the southern edge of the southern sector. Harbord responded to Feland's request for another artillery barrage at 2225hrs by ordering him to consolidate his position and wait until the morning.

Around midnight, in a continued attempt to regain control over the battlefield, Harbord directed Sibley to suspend his offensive, dig in, and defend his hold on the southern portion of Belleau Wood. Two platoons from the 2nd Engineers joined Sibley's 82nd and 83rd companies, while two others moved into Bouresches.

Throughout the night the Marines in Belleau Wood suffered from German gas barrages. The Marines in Bouresches were no better off, enduring both artillery fire and a determined German counterattack at 0230hrs. Dawn found the Marines still holding the town.

As June 6 ended, the 4th Brigade enjoyed a tenuous hold on Hill 142, the southern portions of Belleau Wood and most of Bouresches. The cost of their modest success had been high. On June 6, 1918, the Marines of the 4th Brigade suffered 1,087 dead and wounded, second only to the losses suffered on the first day at Tarawa in November, 1943. The 3rd Brigade's confused movements accounted for over 300 dead and wounded.

Around Château-Thierry, the American 30th Infantry Regiment joined the French 10th Colonial Division in assaulting Hill 204.

June 7, 1918

After midnight Sibley reinforced his position by calling up Capt Egbert Lloyd's 80th Company, which he positioned in the southwest portion of the wood. Capt Phillip Case's 47th and Capt Richard Platt's 20th companies continued to suffer from the Germans on Hill 181 and Sibley hoped Lloyd's fresh troops would be able to drive off the enemy.

At the same time, Harbord ordered Wise's 2/5th, resting in the woods south of Champillon, to move forward and plug the gap between Turrill's position around Hill 142 and Berry's battalion. Wise's men had been under sporadic artillery fire throughout the day. Berry's orders were to take his three companies, Capt Lloyd Williams' 51st Company previously detached, up the Lucy–Torcy road and report to Col Feland. At 0200hrs his battalion moved in single file up the road, through a narrow depression that protected both flanks. About one half-mile from Lucy the ground gave way to sloping fields. Wise halted his men and moved forward cautiously with several squads. After advancing 200 yards rifle fire erupted from the left. Wise shouted over the din that they were Marines. When the fire sputtered to a halt the Americans shouted back that the woods to the right were full of Germans.

The Germans, suspecting a night assault, caught Wise's small group with machine-gun and artillery fire. Wise's group lost half their men as they retreated. Rejoining the remainder of the battalion the Marines retired under fire. Capt John Blanchfield, 55th Company, was killed as the three companies retired, up the slope opposite Belleau Wood, and back into the Champillon Wood. Despite the confused night march and retreat, Wise's men plugged a gaping hole in the American line between Turrill's 1st Battalion around Hill 142 and Berry's decimated command still struggling to advance into the southwest face of Belleau Wood. Although Wise could find no trace of Berry's men on his right, he did contact Conachy's Marines on the left. The Germans subjected Wise and his men to heavy artillery fire. Trench mortars, located in Belleau Wood, added their fire to the pounding of Wise's position.

At 1700hrs, Wise, reacting to orders from Harbord, extended his line to occupy the positions held by Berry's 3/5th. Wise directed the 55th Company, now commanded by Lt Elliot Cooke, to relieve Conachy's 45th Company on the left. Cooke was unable to find Conachy's men and after sending a note to Wise asking for further orders a runner appeared. He said that Conachy had been ordered to occupy a position further forward and he was to lead Cooke to them. The runner led Cooke and his men across a wheatfield filled with dead Marines, to a small wooded area north of Champillon Wood. Cooke deployed his company to defend all approaches to the wood. During the night, the Germans attempted to overrun the Marine position but were driven back. Meanwhile, Berry's shattered battalion was withdrawn to reorganize.

During June 7, the Marines endured constant German artillery fire while they reorganized their positions and gathered their wounded. Sibley's men reinforced their lines in the southern portion of Belleau Wood, while in Bouresches Holcomb's men settled down to defend the town. Harbord, still lacking a complete and accurate picture of the battlefield, suggested in a report to Bundy that he might withdraw troops from Bouresches. He also mused that he wanted to straighten out his line by capturing a rectangle of woods east of Hill 142. Most troubling, he still underestimated German strength inside Belleau Wood and ordered Sibley to prepare for a dawn assault on June 8.

On the far right of the 2nd Division, the 9th Regiment moved cautiously forward beyond the hamlet of Monneaux. To their right, the French 10th Colonial Division ran into fresh enemy and settled down on the slope of Hill 204. The position occupied by the 9th Regiment, which included the Bois de la Marette, would remain virtually unchanged for the next several weeks.

French intelligence concluded that German pressure along the Montdidier–Noyon sector had lessened as reinforcements were moved to deal with the American attack on Belleau Wood. The French determined that the 5th Prussian Guard Division was coming into the line to replace the 197th Division, and the 28th Division was moving to relieve the 10th Division. Both the 5th Prussians and 28th Division were first rate combat units.

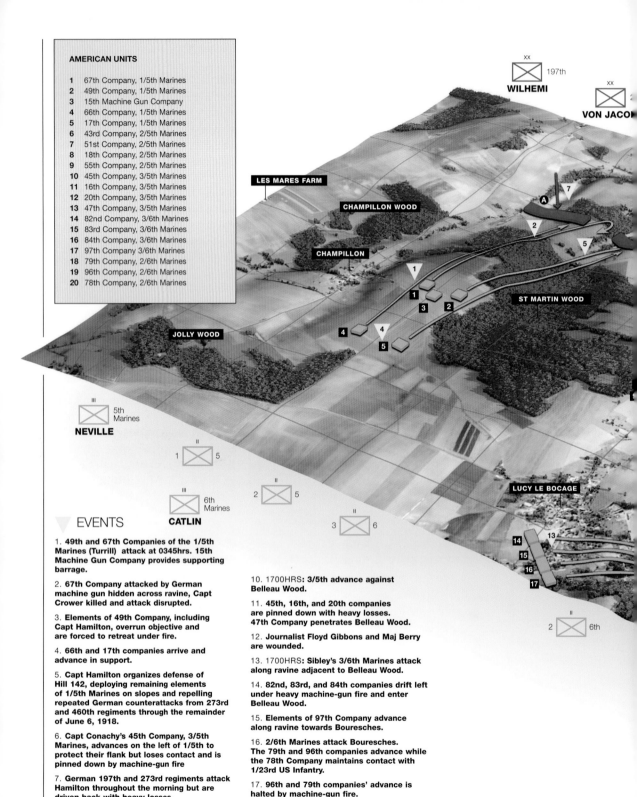

AMERICAN UNITS

1	67th Company, 1/5th Marines
2	49th Company, 1/5th Marines
3	15th Machine Gun Company
4	66th Company, 1/5th Marines
5	17th Company, 1/5th Marines
6	43rd Company, 2/5th Marines
7	51st Company, 2/5th Marines
8	18th Company, 2/5th Marines
9	55th Company, 2/5th Marines
10	45th Company, 3/5th Marines
11	16th Company, 3/5th Marines
12	20th Company, 3/5th Marines
13	47th Company, 3/5th Marines
14	82nd Company, 3/6th Marines
15	83rd Company, 3/6th Marines
16	84th Company, 3/6th Marines
17	97th Company 3/6th Marines
18	79th Company, 2/6th Marines
19	96th Company, 2/6th Marines
20	78th Company, 2/6th Marines

WILHEMI

197th

VON JACO

LES MARES FARM

CHAMPILLON WOOD

CHAMPILLON

ST MARTIN WOOD

JOLLY WOOD

5th Marines

NEVILLE

1 — 5

6th Marines

CATLIN

2 — 5

3 — 6

LUCY LE BOCAGE

2 — 6th

▼ EVENTS

1. **49th and 67th Companies of the 1/5th Marines (Turrill) attack at 0345hrs. 15th Machine Gun Company provides supporting barrage.**

2. **67th Company attacked by German machine gun hidden across ravine, Capt Crower killed and attack disrupted.**

3. **Elements of 49th Company, including Capt Hamilton, overrun objective and are forced to retreat under fire.**

4. **66th and 17th companies arrive and advance in support.**

5. **Capt Hamilton organizes defense of Hill 142, deploying remaining elements of 1/5th Marines on slopes and repelling repeated German counterattacks from 273rd and 460th regiments through the remainder of June 6, 1918.**

6. **Capt Conachy's 45th Company, 3/5th Marines, advances on the left of 1/5th to protect their flank but loses contact and is pinned down by machine-gun fire**

7. **German 197th and 273rd regiments attack Hamilton throughout the morning but are driven back with heavy losses.**

8. **Two battalions of the 5th Guard Division are sent to reinforce the 273rd Regiment.**

9. **Three platoons from Conachy's 45th Company join the rest of 3/5th Marines for assault on Belleau Wood.**

10. 1700HRS**: 3/5th advance against Belleau Wood.**

11. **45th, 16th, and 20th companies are pinned down with heavy losses. 47th Company penetrates Belleau Wood.**

12. **Journalist Floyd Gibbons and Maj Berry are wounded.**

13. 1700HRS**: Sibley's 3/6th Marines attack along ravine adjacent to Belleau Wood.**

14. **82nd, 83rd, and 84th companies drift left under heavy machine-gun fire and enter Belleau Wood.**

15. **Elements of 97th Company advance along ravine towards Bouresches.**

16. **2/6th Marines attack Bouresches. The 79th and 96th companies advance while the 78th Company maintains contact with 1/23rd US Infantry.**

17. **96th and 79th companies' advance is halted by machine-gun fire.**

18. **Lt Cates of the 96th Company leads remainder of his platoon into the shelter of the ravine and captures Bouresches. Americans repulse attacks by elements of German 10th Division over the next several days.**

JUNE 6 ATTACKS

The 4th Brigade of the US 2nd Division began large-scale offensive operations in the early morning of June 6, 1918. At 0345hrs the 1/5th Marines attacked the German 460th and 273rd regiments and captured Hill 142. At 1700hrs the 2/5th Marines attacked the western portion of Belleau Wood suffering heavy casualties. At the same time the 3/6th Marines advanced into the eastern side of Belleau Wood and elements of 2/6th Marines captured the village of Bouresches. Although the Marines would strengthen their hold on Bouresches, heavy casualties would cause them to withdraw from Belleau Wood.

Note: Gridlines are shown at intervals of 500 m (546 yds)

GERMAN UNITS

A	273rd Regiment
B	460th Regiment
C	1/461st Regiment
D	2/461st Regiment
E	3/461st Regiment
F	398th Regiment

Officers of the Marine 4th
Brigade at religious services
inside Belleau Wood.

June 8, 1918

During the night, Sibley began to organize his men for the attack. Sibley intended to use the 82nd and 83rd companies, reinforced by two platoons of the 80th Company, to attack. Adapting to the costly futility of the previous day's advance in dressed lines and the broken terrain, Sibley ordered the Marines to move in skirmish lines. Stokes mortars and supplies of hand grenades were brought up to support the attack. The 2nd Engineers, commanded by Capt Dederer, were assigned to move up the eastern edge of the wood and protect the right flank. During the night, Dederer withdrew the two platoons of engineers in Bouresches. As Sibley's men were redeploying, the Germans unleashed a furious barrage on the American positions in the wood and along the line held by the 23rd Regiment. German infantry followed the artillery, probing for a weak spot in the American line. The Germans bounced first off the Marines, then the 23rd Regiment, before glancing off the 9th Regiment.

At 0400hrs the Marines surged forward, only to be driven to ground by German machine guns. Progress was measured by yards and at 0600hrs Sibley ordered in the 84th Company and had several 37mm guns brought forward to support the attack. By 0800hrs, the entire line was pinned down and Sibley sent Harbord a pessimistic note, writing "these machine guns are too strong for our infantry." Around noon, Harbord ordered Sibley to retire to the ravine along the southern edge of the wood, while American artillery pummeled the German positions. At the same time two companies from the 461st Regiment and an engineer company attacked the Marines, taking 40 prisoners.

At about 2200hrs, Lee informed Sibley that his battered battalion was to move out of the wood into reserve around Paris Farm. Sibley's men moved out, leaving the 84th Company to cover their withdrawal. Harbord informed Maj John Hughes, 1/6th Marines, that he should move his battalion from their positions around Paris Farm to relieve Sibley's men.

Maj Maurice Shearer was given command of Berry's 3/5th and told by Harbord to familiarize himself with Bouresches in preparation for his command to relieve Holcomb's men on the night of June 9. Although Harbord had initially intended for Maj John A. Hughes' command to replace Sibley, he later decided to subject the Germans in Belleau Wood to an intense bombardment before ordering another attack. During the evening replacements arrived at the front and were distributed among the units that had seen their ranks decimated over the past several days.

Despite Ludendorff's claim that "in spite of a few unavoidable temporary crises, our troops remain masters of the situation, both in attack and defense," on June 8, he issued an order to all Army groups, directing that "American units appearing on the front should be hit particularly hard in order to render difficult the formation of an American Army." Although Ludendorff correctly assessed the insignificant tactical gains resulting from the American attacks of June 6 and 7, he failed to fully recognize the greater importance. The local commanders facing the Americans had a much clearer understanding of the challenge before them.

An intelligence report issued by the German 28th Division on June 8 identified the elements of the 2nd Division but concluded that, after the attacks of June 6 and 7, the division "is probably no longer very efficient." The report went on to correctly conclude that the Allies would use the success of the Americans in stopping the German advance for propaganda purposes. The report concluded by asserting:

> *Should the Americans on our front gain the upper hand only temporarily, this may have the most unfortunate influence on the morale of the entente and on the continuation of the war. In the fighting that faces us it is therefore not a matter of the possession or non-possession of a village or wood of indifferent value of itself, but the question of whether the English-American publicity will succeed in representing the American Army as one equal to the German Army or as actually superior troops.*

The battle of Belleau Wood had taken on an importance much greater than the simple possession of the blood-stained ground.

June 9, 1918

Ludendorff attacked again on June 9, in the Montdidier–Noyon sector. He needed to expand the salient he had driven into the French lines, but his timetable for launching this offensive had been thrown off by the American resistance around Château-Thierry and Belleau Wood, allowing the French to strengthen their lines. Over the next two days the Germans achieved some territorial advantage, driving a narrow seven-mile finger six or so miles into the French lines. Despite the initial success, the Germans' position was becoming untenable. The German commander, Gen von Hutier, had weakened his flanks to concentrate his forces in the center. Once the advance ground to a halt the French took advantage of the German weakness and on June 11, five fresh French divisions cleared the Aronde valley of German forces, capturing over 1,000 Germans.

The 1/6th, marching without Maj Hughes, became lost as it moved forward and as day broke found itself under German artillery fire. The battalion sought shelter nearby in a small wood and settled down for the day. Meanwhile, American and French artillery began a systematic pummeling of the Germans, throwing 28,000 75mm and 6,000 155mm shells into Belleau Wood. In return, the Germans shelled Bouresches, Lucy, and suspected concentration areas in the rear throughout the day.

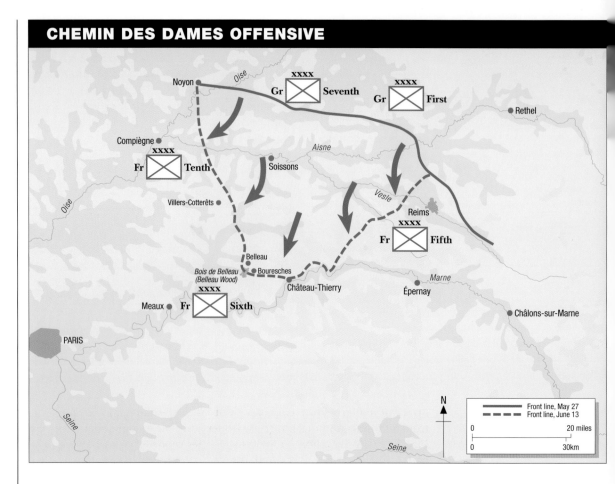

With nightfall, Hughes' men resumed their movement to their jump-off positions. Hughes carried with him an order from Harbord to begin an attack on the southern portion of Belleau Wood at 0430hrs on June 10. Throughout the day the battalions shattered in the preceding day's attacks received replacements, still dressed in the Marine forest-green uniforms.

June 10, 1918

As Hughes was moving into position to attack, Gen von Conta was reshuffling his forces to make good their losses. On his right he replaced the 197th Division with the 5th Guards Division, while on the left the 28th Division took over from the 10th Division. Most importantly, von Conta shifted his division sectors to the right. Responsibility for defending Belleau Wood was now split between Bischoff and elements of the 28th Division. 28th Division commander, Gen von Boehn, deployed two regiments in line and one in reserve. The 40th Fusiliers were positioned on the right and were responsible for defending Belleau Wood. They placed two battalions in line, one facing Bouresches and one in Belleau Wood. The third battalion was deployed in reserve. The commander of the 2/40th Fusiliers spread two companies across the 500-yard defensive line which Bischoff had defended with six companies. Bischoff, whose 461st Regiment was now assigned to defend a smaller portion of the western edge of the wood, protested to no avail. Maj von Hartlieb's 1/461st was given the task of defending the wood.

Hughes' 1/6th, joined by the 77th and 23rd Machine Gun companies, jumped off at 0430hrs, following the rolling barrage which stalked slowly north. Unlike the previous attacks, which were broken as they began, Hughes advanced quickly. At about 0700hrs, Hughes reported to Lee that a machine-gun position in the northeast portion of the wood was holding up Capt Fuller's 75th Company, but he was sending in a couple of trench mortars and machine guns under Maj Cole, commander of the 6th Machine Gun Battalion. At 0800hrs Hughes reported that Cole had been badly wounded and evacuated. He also notified Harbord that he had made good progress with very few losses. Hughes had overestimated how much ground he had taken and Harbord, desperate to believe that the Marines had finally cracked the hard nut of Belleau, began making plans for the complete capture of the wood. In reality, Hughes was some 800 yards south of where Harbord expected.

Harbord met with Col Wise and told him he expected him to capture the northern portion of the wood and, working in conjunction with Hughes on his right, sweep through to Bouresches. He also told Wise that he was free to make his own plans for the offensive. In one of the more curious and enduring mysteries of the Belleau Wood campaign, Wise claimed to have devised a bold plan to attack the Germans from the flank and rear by marching north of Hill 169. Wise also contended that he had the full support of his company commanders and had consulted Maj Hughes, who readily supported the proposal. Wise was distraught when, sometime during the night of June 10–11, he received an order from Harbord directing him to assault the section of Belleau Wood directly to his front, across open fields, preceded by a rolling barrage. Rather than undertake a flanking movement that could have minimized casualties and broken the German hold on Belleau Wood, Wise was ordered, as Berry and Holcomb were before him, to advance headlong into a storm of German machine guns. Although Wise claimed that all four company commanders supported his idea, one later suggested that "we held out for the frontal attack. We didn't want any razzle dazzle, but a direct power play with plenty of artillery."

73

During the lull in fighting, the 5th Guards Division relieved the 197th Division, while the 10th Division was relieved by the 28th Division.

June 11, 1918

At 0400hrs, Wise's 2/5th, deployed in an "artillery formation" with two companies forward and two behind, watched as American and French artillery pummeled the field and wood's edge. Behind the barrage the battalion moved steadily towards the wood. Capt Charles Dunbeck's 43rd was on the left, followed by Capt Lester Wass's 18th Company. On the right, Williams' 51st was followed by Cooke's 55th. German machine-gun fire riddled the line, but Wise's men plunged into the wood. Despite the intention to advance in a northeasterly direction, aiming for the northern portion of the wood, Wise's men struck out towards the southeast, confused perhaps by the early morning darkness, a heavy mist, and the smoke created by the barrage.

Wise's men found well-camouflaged machine-gun positions deployed to provide support to each other, and snipers hidden among the rock out-croppings and in the trees. Progress was slow and costly. As previously agreed, Hughes directed a company to maintain contact with Wise's movement, but in the thick woods and underbrush that proved difficult. By noon, Wise had received a steady stream of reports detailing the capture of German positions and made his way into the wood. He found that Capt Williams was dead, as were many junior officers. He spoke to his other company commanders and found that the Marines had redeployed the captured German machine guns to guard against an expected counterattack. As the attack stalled, the supporting companies bunched up with those leading the attack. Both the 18th and 55th moved to the left of the leading companies and the battalion found itself in a line.

The 2/5th's right hit the German 40th Regiment, which had relieved the 462nd Regiment as part of von Conta's ill-advised shifting of divisional boundaries. The 40th was shattered, losing over 700 men, and retreated towards the eastern portion of the wood. A later report claimed that the Marines attacked in:

…gangs of ten to twenty men, primed with alcohol. Some of their wounded keep on in the attack. Our men threw hand grenades into these gangs but were simply ignored by the enemy. They had no idea of tactical principles. They fired while walking with their rifles under their arms. They carried light machine guns with them … no hand grenades but knives, revolvers, rifle butts and bayonets. All were big fellows, powerful rowdies.

Hughes' 1/6th failed to tie into Wise's right during the advance and that gap allowed several German machine guns to plague Wise's rear throughout the morning. Despite his losses, Wise believed he had achieved his objective and overly optimistic reports from some company officers only reinforced the confusion. Wise sent Harbord a note based on his erroneous belief, claiming "Belleau Wood belongs to the 5th Marines."

On the Marines' left the 461st Regiment gave some ground but increased resistance throughout the day. Von Hartlieb's 1/461st, reinforced with two companies from the 2/461st, held the line. Bischoff kept several companies in reserve near the hunting lodge in the northwest corner of the wood. The Marine attack overwhelmed two German companies and forced two others to retreat. Bischoff responded by calling up his reserve companies. Early in the afternoon an additional battalion from the 110th Regiment, 28th Division, filtered into the wood to stiffen the line.

The Marine company commanders held a brief meeting in the wood to determine their next move. They were joined by Lt Matthews, battalion intelligence officer, who had just returned from a reconnaissance of the northwest section of the wood. Matthews was unable to convince the company commanders that the town to their front was Bouresches, not Belleau. When Matthews reported that the woods to the left were full of Germans, Wise turned on him, calling him a "goddamned young bonehead" who didn't know what he was talking about. Wise would later unfairly relieve Matthews as intelligence officer.

Wise also received a note that Capt Alphonse de Carre, with the 5th Marine headquarters company, was assigned to provide support to Wise. They advanced sometime after Wise jumped off. De Carre advanced along the intended direction, into the northern section of the wood, and captured 180 Germans. De Carre reported that area of the wood full of the enemy.

Despite growing evidence to the contrary, including the eyewitness accounts from Matthews, Wise and his company commanders continued to believe that they had advanced into the northern portion of the wood. Based on this mistake Wise continued to send triumphant notes to Harbord, who passed them on to Bundy, who in turn sent a telegram to Pershing. The next day the *New York Times* boasted of the American success and newspapers across the country trumpeted that the Marines had stopped the Germans.

Shearer, now defending Bouresches, requested artillery support to break up an attempt by the reserve company of the 2/40th Fusiliers to reinforce Belleau Wood. Neville responded to Wise's reports of heavy casualties by requesting two companies of engineers to reinforce Wise. Wise now realized that his message to Harbord announcing Belleau Wood clear of the enemy was somewhat premature. Around noon he sent a

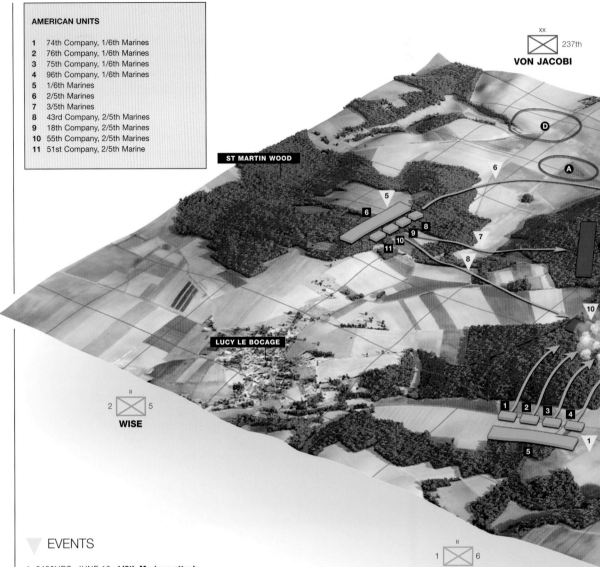

AMERICAN UNITS

1 74th Company, 1/6th Marines
2 76th Company, 1/6th Marines
3 75th Company, 1/6th Marines
4 96th Company, 1/6th Marines
5 1/6th Marines
6 2/5th Marines
7 3/5th Marines
8 43rd Company, 2/5th Marines
9 18th Company, 2/5th Marines
10 55th Company, 2/5th Marines
11 51st Company, 2/5th Marine

VON JACOBI

ST MARTIN WOOD

LUCY LE BOCAGE

WISE

HUGHES

▼ EVENTS

1. 0430HRS, JUNE 10: **1/6th Marines attack. German machine-gun nests and the tangled landscape of Belleau Wood slow the advance.**

2. **German defense of Belleau Wood has been split between the 461st Regiment and the 40th Fusilier Regiment.**

3. **12 Hotchkiss machine guns fire a curtain barrage between Bouresches and Belleau Wood to block German reinforcements.**

4. **Col Hughes and the 1/6th are stopped short of their objective.**

5. **Col Wise is ordered to prepare the 2/5th to attack Belleau Wood. Wise aligns his battalion for the attack. His objective is to capture the northern portion of the wood and join with Hughes' 1/6th to clear the Germans.**

6. **Wise suggests a flanking movement to enter the wood from the north. This movement would have brought his 2/5th Marines into the rear of the German defenses.**

7. **Although Wise believes his plan had been approved and begins preparations for the flanking movement, he receives orders from Brig Gen Harbord directing him to conduct a direct assault on the German defenses.**

8. 0440HRS, JUNE 11: **Wise's advance drifts south and enters the wood on the flank of the German 2/40th Fusiliers, which is routed and retreats north. The 461st Regiment retires but keeps pressure on Wise's left flank.**

9. **The 43rd Company (Dunbeck) reaches the eastern edge of Belleau Wood and incorrectly reports all objectives taken. Dunbeck's men have not captured the northern portion of the Wood but have merely occupied the area intended as the objective of Hughes' 1/6th on June 10.**

10. **Col Hughes' 1/6th continues to push north against the 2/40th in conjunction with Wise's attack. Hughes fails to connect his left with Wise's right, allowing the Germans to harass the rear of Wise's battalion throughout the day.**

JUNE 10–11 ATTACKS

The 1/6th Marines advance into Belleau Wood in the early morning of June 10, 1918 but run into heavy machine-gun fire. Suffering heavy casualties the 1/6th achieves a modest advance. General Harbord orders the 2/5th Marines to attack into the western edge of Belleau Wood early on June 11 to support Hughes. The 2/5th attack becomes disoriented, penetrating Belleau Wood well south of their objective.

Note: Gridlines are shown at intervals of 500m (546 yds)

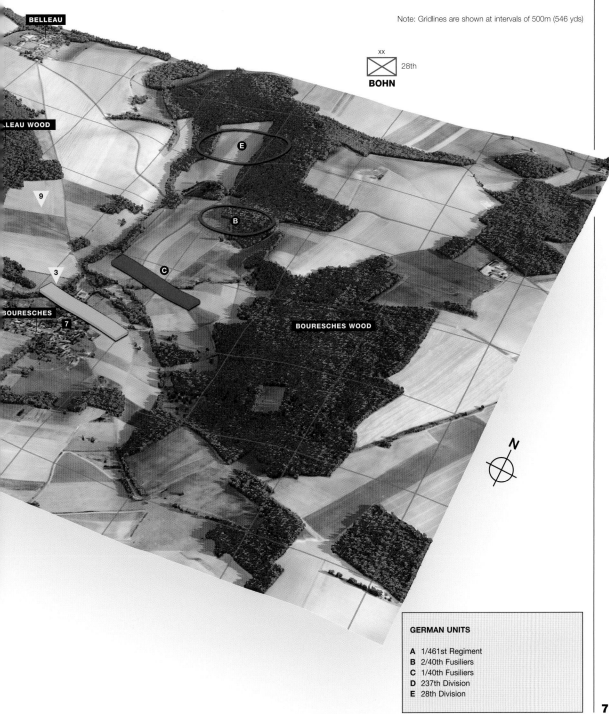

BELLEAU

LEAU WOOD

BOURESCHES

BOURESCHES WOOD

xx
28th
BOHN

GERMAN UNITS

A 1/461st Regiment
B 2/40th Fusiliers
C 1/40th Fusiliers
D 237th Division
E 28th Division

77

short note to Harbord declaring that "my left flank is weak." Now alert to the threat to his left flank, he conferred with Maj Hughes and requested a company from the 1/6th to move into the northern section of the wood. Although Hughes readily agreed, Harbord notified Wise that he intended to use artillery to neutralize any German threat to his flank. Matthews, still arguing that the German threat on the left was real, suggested that Wise commit the 74th Company to the left. Wise agreed and also directed Cooke and the 55th Company to move from the right to the left.

A patrol, headed by Capt Cooke, moved north through the destruction and found German reinforcements deploying along a new defensive line. Realizing that the 2/5th was now in danger of being rolled up from a flank attack, Cooke moved his company, 80 or so men, perpendicular to the line held by Wass's 18th Company and Lt Drinkard Milner, who replaced the wounded Dunbeck and now commanded the 43rd Company. Cooke estimated that the 51st Company had no more than 16 men. When 75 replacements showed up looking for the front line, Cooke pointed east and replied, "It's there," then pointed north, "and there ... and pretty soon if we don't look out it's going to be there."

The day ended with Wise still unsure of either his exact location or the full extent of his losses. In turn, Harbord and higher command continued to believe that the Marines had the situation well in hand, despite messages from Wise requesting assistance. As they settled down for the night, the Marines integrated the replacements into the battered companies and continued to fight off small probes from German patrols.

At about this time, Harbord began sending messages to Bundy noting that the Marine brigade had been engaged in continuous fighting for over a week and needed to be relieved. He wrote:

Officers and men are now at a state scarcely less than complete physical exhaustion. Men fall asleep under bombardment and the physical exhaustion and the heavy losses are a combination calculated to damage morale, which should be met by immediate arrangements for the relief of the brigade.

While there was no immediate chance of relief, Pershing's staff was now alert to the deteriorating situation.

June 12, 1918

Early in the morning, Harbord, Neville, and Feland, aided by Wise's own suggestion that he could capture the remainder of the wood if assisted by artillery, ordered another attack for 1700hrs. It was to be preceded by an artillery barrage on the northeastern portion of the wood. The decision to attack seems to have been driven in part by a belief that Wise was much further north and only a small section of the wood needed to be captured. More importantly, Harbord, having announced to Pershing and the world that his men had captured Belleau Wood, needed to make that happen.

Wise spent the day duly arranging his attack while his men endured intense German bombardment. Cooke, Milner, and Wass were slated to advance supported by what remained of Williams' company. Hughes' 1/6th would follow. Predictably the artillery, targeted just beyond the areas everyone assumed Wise occupied, fell too far north and did little damage to the German line of resistance. Wise noted that the artillery seemed light and asked that it be extended until 1730hrs.

Wise's men stepped into a maelstrom of German fire. The short-comings of parade-ground tactics had not been lost on the Marine veterans and they advanced, as described by Wise, "red Indian style," in small groups. Machine guns, snipers, and grenades all took their toll. Despite their losses the Marines overran the initial German line and surged into the reserve line. The Marine cry of "Eee-yah-yip," learned during training at Paris Island and Quantico, echoed through the wood. The German line broke and survivors streamed back to the north.

On the left, 43rd Company under Lt Milner somehow advanced across Cooke's front, formed the leftmost element of the American line, and occupied the hunting lodge, capturing a large group of Germans. Cooke continued up the middle, while on the right Wass reached the northeast corner. Milner, told by a captured German officer to expect a counterattack, moved his command to the right to tie into Cooke's men. In turn Cooke moved towards Wass and Wass reached out to his right to connect with Hughes. While this general contraction strengthened the Marine line it resulted in a gradual shift to the right, further exposing the left flank.

The Marine assault had shattered the battalion from the German 110th Regiment and again pushed back the 461st into the northwest corner of the wood. As the Marines sidled to the right, the remaining Germans followed close behind. The end of the American left faced to the east and came to rest along a small rocky knoll, creating what would be known as "the Hook." Company F, 2nd Engineers, sent forward to support Wise, started out with 185 men. The engineers were caught in a German barrage of high explosives and gas that killed their commander and dispersed the company. Only 50 men reached Wass.

Wise informed Harbord that his men were in a precarious position and might not be able to withstand a determined counterattack. In two days, Wise's men had captured over 60 machine guns, ten trench mortars and over 400 prisoners. The price had been high. Wise estimated that, despite recent replacements, he had merely 300 men left in his battalion, a 70 percent casualty rate. Early in the evening, Harbord began to issue orders intended to provide some relief to his depleted units. Sibley's 3/6th was ordered to relieve Turrill's 1/5th on Hill 142. Turrill received

CLASH OF PATROLS, JUNE 14, 1918 (pages 80–81)

On June 12, 1918 the 2/5th Marines attacked the German line defending the northern portion of Belleau Wood. Although they successfully scattered the German defenders the Marines suffered significant casualties and could not defend the broad front they had captured. Although the Marines contracted their lines, their left flank was hanging in the air. Captain Cooke, commanding the 55th Company, refused his flank and created "the Hook." The German 461st Regiment, which had retreated during the initial attack quickly noted the vulnerability of the Marine flank and began to probe the American lines. In response to repeated German penetrations, on June 14, 1918 Captain Cooke ordered a small patrol to establish contact with the Germans. At the same time a German patrol was feeling its way through the dense forest and collided with Cooke's Marines. A desperate hand-to-hand melee resulted in the Marines driving off the Germans and capturing several prisoners. This section of the Wood had suffered from severe artillery fire, shredding the trees (1) and further limiting visibility. In this confined battlefield hand grenades (2) were effective weapons. The Chauchat light machine gunner (3) and his assistant found few targets in the confused hand-to-hand combat where the Marines excelled with the bayonet (4). Most of the Marines had worn out their original forest green uniforms, replacing them with Army issued khaki (5). Some Marines continued to wear a mix of uniforms (6) and officers tended to wear their original standard issue forest green for longer periods (7). Throughout the battle for Belleau Wood the weather was hot and dry, resulting in the American infantry shedding their jackets in favor of shirts (8). To distinguish themselves from regular army units the Marines wore a small brass globe and anchor insignia on their helmets (9). Small unit encounters like these continued throughout the next several weeks until the Marines cleared Belleau Wood.

over 100 replacements and was placed in St Martin Wood with orders to protect against a German thrust along the western edge of the wood.

Just before midnight, 4th Brigade intelligence suggested that the Germans were planning a major counterattack. Intense German artillery fire throughout the night confirmed their estimate.

June 13, 1918

Early on the 13th, the Germans began probing the American lines. German artillery then began to saturate the wood with high explosives and gas. During the early morning Holcomb was ordered to occupy the southern portion of St Martin Wood as a reserve. Before Holcomb could complete this move Harbord ordered his 79th and 80th companies into the ravine south of Belleau Wood, responding to renewed German pressure on Bouresches. Elements of the 109th Grenadier Regiment and 40th Fusiliers advanced against Bouresches. The Fusiliers started their assault late and heavy machine-gun fire broke up their attack in the fields outside the town. Although the German attack failed, a false report that the town had been overrun by Germans caused Harbord to redirect part of Holcomb's battalion. Holcomb continued on to St Martin with his remaining two companies. Shearer belatedly informed Harbord that the Marines still held Bouresches.

After Wise reported his line was holding, Harbord determined that his immediate goal would be to connect Wise's left with Turrill's right. After establishing his battalion in St Martin Wood, Turrill ordered Capt Roswell Winans' 17th Company to make contact with Wise's left flank somewhere in the northwest portion of Belleau Wood. Winans spent the morning sending patrols into the wood but found only dead Marines

American medics tending to a wounded officer on the battlefield. German prisoners were used to carry the wounded to rear areas.

and pockets of Germans. After being spotted by a German airplane, Winans pulled his men back across the Lucy–Torcy road just before German artillery raked his previous location. Winans reported to Turrill that Wise was nowhere near the western edge of Belleau Wood.

Late in the afternoon of June 13, Harbord issued Field Order Number Five, directing a battalion from the 23rd Infantry to relieve Shearer's 3/5th in Bouresches. Holcomb's 2/6th was ordered to replace Wise. Responding to a lack of cooperation between Wise and Hughes, Harbord attempted to establish greater command control over the intermixed units. He assigned Lt Col Lee responsibility for the left section of the line, while Col Neville would oversee the right. The boundary extended roughly north–south through the middle of Belleau Wood.

The intent of the shifting of troops was to reduce the area to be defended by the 4th Brigade, while extending the 3rd Brigade's area of responsibility. The 9th Regiment now held a line from Monneaux to the woods north of Le Thiolet. The 23rd Regiment extended from Le Thiolet to Bouresches. The relief was slated to begin early on June 14.

June 14, 1918

Holcomb gathered up his dispersed companies and prepared to move forward just after midnight. German artillery fire had been steady throughout the previous afternoon and evening. Just as they moved forward, the Germans unleashed a massive barrage of gas into the middle and southern section of the wood. Holcomb's men were driven to ground and forced to endure high explosive fire while wearing their cumbersome gas masks. Hughes' battalion was also subjected to the gas attack. The 74th Company was destroyed and Hughes was wounded and replaced by Maj Franklin Garrett. Casualties were extensive in both battalions and Holcomb reported to Wise with only about half his command. The 96th and 78th companies were decimated and the survivors evacuated. The 23rd Infantry also suffered 150 casualties as it moved up to replace Shearer in Bouresches. Wise's men were spared the gas, but fought off a German attack at about 0130hrs.

Rather than replace Wise, what was left of Holcomb's command was integrated into the defensive line along with the survivors of Hughes' battalion. Hughes' 80th Company was redeployed on Wise's left, further strengthening the vulnerable hook. Things had gone from bad to worse for Harbord. Recognizing that lack of central command was adding to the problems, Harbord assigned Lt Col Feland authority over all the Marines in Belleau Wood. Feland arrived at Wise's command post at 1500hrs and after a quick reconnaissance his assistant, Maj Ralph Keyser, pronounced the northwest section of the wood full of Germans. Feland then conferred with Turrill and decided to accompany Winans on another attempt to contact Wise's left flank. At the same time, Harbord informed Holcomb that his battalion was going back in.

June 15, 1918

On June 15, French Gen Degoutte was promoted to command the French Sixth Army. Degoutte had resolutely refused repeated requests from Gen Bundy and his chief of staff to relieve the 4th Brigade. Degoutte had maintained that the 3rd Brigade should replace the 4th, but Bundy refused. Degoutte's successor, Gen Nauline, continued to suggest the 3rd Brigade be used in relief. The Americans suggested that the 7th Infantry, 3rd Division, was in reserve and should be reassigned to assist the 3rd Brigade. Although Nauline initially rejected the suggestion, Bundy's threat, as senior American commander in the sector, to assume command of all American units changed his mind.

Early in the morning, Winans and the 17th Company attacked the northeast section of Belleau Wood, supported by 37mm guns, Stokes mortars, and machine-gun fire. Winans was wounded but his men, reinforced by Turrill, pushed back Hartlieb's men. Winans' men finally made contact on their right with Wise and tied in with Case's 20th Company in the St Martin Wood, reestablishing a continuous line.

Feland reported to Harbord that German resistance in the wood seemed isolated to 60 or so men with several machine guns defending a small rocky knoll in the northwestern corner of the wood. Lt Col Adams, 1/7th, and several officers arrived to coordinate the relief of the Marines. Feland rejected a suggestion to make one last effort to clear the wood, claiming that his men were exhausted, the German position was weak, and that Adams could finish the job once the relief was completed.

After dark, the 7th Infantry began their relief of the Marines. One battalion would replace its counterpart each night to avoid arousing notice from the Germans. Only the Marine 3/5th remained in the wood. The Germans were relieved to see them go. An official report, prepared on June 16 by Conta Corps staff, described the Marines:

> They are healthy, strong, physically well set up men from eighteen to twenty-eight years old, who at present, lack only the necessary training to make them a dangerous foe. The spirit of the troops is high and they possess an innocent self confidence. A characteristic expression of the prisoners is, 'we kill or get killed'.

The Germans, too, were suffering from horrendous casualties and the front-line units were in need of relief. On June 4, the 237th Division fielded 3,200 men. By June 13, the division was reduced to just over 1,500 men. The 87th Division, a fourth class unit, was assigned to Conta's Corps on June 14. At the same time as the Marines were withdrawing, the 87th Division was moving 1/347th Regiment into Belleau Wood. A second battalion was deployed in close support and the third placed in reserve. The Germans deployed three companies in Belleau Wood and the fourth in reserve in the village of Belleau. During the lull, the Germans established a more complete system of trenches and machine-gun emplacements in their small corner of the wood, although the local commander still considered his position precarious.

While the Marines tried to recuperate, Wise and Harbord exchanged angry words over Wise's inaccurate reports. Wise correctly surmised that Harbord's anger had more to do with embarrassment with his superiors than it did with the accuracy of the reports. Wise suggested that if Harbord had doubts about the reports "why hadn't anybody from brigade headquarters come down to take a look for themselves."

The next several days were relatively quiet, reinforcing a misguided notion among the officers of the 7th that the battle for Belleau Wood was all but over. Nevertheless, the 7th Infantry diligently went about their work with the help of the 2nd Engineers, improving their defensive positions,

stringing barbed wire, and sending out patrols. Meanwhile, the 1/7th faced the Germans continuing to hold the northwest corner of Belleau Wood.

June 20, 1918

On June 20, Harbord ordered 1/7th commander, Lt Col John Adams, to push the Germans out of their positions in the corner of Belleau Wood. The planned attack misfired, with only two of the planned force of four platoons advancing. The reinforced Germans drove the inexperienced Americans back with heavy casualties.

Harbord ordered Adams to try again the next day. Harbord agreed to Adams' request for strong artillery support. Just before companies A and B were to advance, Adams and his staff noted that the barrage was light and ineffective. Company B got lost in the unfamiliar wood and fell behind. Company A attacked as planned at 0400hrs and lost about 180 men to German artillery and machine-gun fire. The repulse led to erroneous reports of German infiltration on the flank and rear. It also resulted in uncorroborated stories of Germans in American uniforms giving contradictory orders. In their brief stay in Belleau Wood, the 7th Regiment suffered over 300 casualties, mostly in the 1st Battalion.

June 22, 1918

Harbord had no choice but to call on 3/5th Marines, in brigade reserve, to restore order. Maj Shearer, who had rejoined his command, sent the 47th Company to investigate the reports of a German breakthrough around Hill 169. They found nothing. Harbord attributed the failure of the 7th Infantry to capture the "little machine-gun nest" to poor leadership and inadequate training. He ordered Shearer to relieve the 1/7th that evening. As Shearer was settling into his new position, a deserter from the 3rd Reserve Ersatz Regiment, 87th Division, described the German positions in the northern portion of the wood as substantial. Reconnaissance by Lt Col Feland confirmed the Americans' worst suspicions. Harbord still instructed Shearer to prepare to capture the woods by 2200hrs the next day with no artillery preparation.

At the same time as Shearer was considering how to push the last Germans out of the wood, other Marine units were ordered back into Belleau Wood. Sibley and 3/6th would relieve 2/7th, and Wise with the 2/5th would relieve the 3/7th. Holcomb and the 2/6th would be placed in brigade reserve around Lucy. Hughes with the 1/6th and Turrill's 1/5th would be in the Bois Gros Jean as division reserve. During their short rest, all the depleted Marine units had received replacements, although none of the units returned to the line at full strength.

June 23, 1918
The 4th Brigade now held a line anchored on the left at Hill 142. The 2/5th held the line from Hill 142 to the Lucy–Torcy road. The battalion was now commanded by Maj Keyser after Harbord relieved Wise from command of the 2/5th. Shearer's men stretched across the northern portion of the wood and tied into Sibley's battalion, which extended to Bouresches, still defended by the 23rd.

Shearer deployed his battalion in a single line, 45th, 16th, 20th, and 47th companies from left to right. At 1900hrs the battalion plunged back into action, supported by mortar and heavy machine-gun fire. The Marines pushed back the German forward line, noting that several machine-gun crews retired with their guns as the Marines approached. After gaining merely 200 yards, Shearer's men retired under German artillery back to their start line. Gaining about 200 yards cost Shearer over 130 casualties.

June 24, 1918
Responding to Shearer's post-battle assessment that something more would be needed to dislodge the Germans, a meeting was arranged involving Harbord, Bundy, division artillery officer Brig Gen William Chamberlaine, Neville, and the 4th Brigade battalion commanders. At the meeting it was agreed to pull back the Marines and unleash the artillery on the Germans. Chamberlaine's guns were supplemented by French light and heavy batteries. A total of 18 batteries opened fire at 0300hrs and blasted the wood until 1700hrs.

June 25, 1918
At 1700hrs Shearer's men attacked again. Resistance was stiff, but the artillery barrage had reduced the effectiveness of the machine guns and by 1900hrs Shearer reported that the 20th and 47th companies had reached their objectives and were digging in. The 16th Company had run into strong resistance but was making progress. Shearer requested support from Keyser's battalion and reminded Harbord that efforts should be made to mop up remaining resistance in the area over which his men had advanced. Harbord directed Sibley to send Shearer two platoons. To assist the 16th Company, still struggling on the left, Keyser was ordered to move to the right. American and French artillery fire was shifted to disperse small units of Germans trying to reorganize near the Lucy–Torcy road.

The commander of the 1/347th responded to the Marine attack by ordering up his reserve company and requesting the release of the 3/347th. Rather than release the reserve battalion, divisional staff directed the 3rd Reserve Ersatz Regiment to provide two companies. It

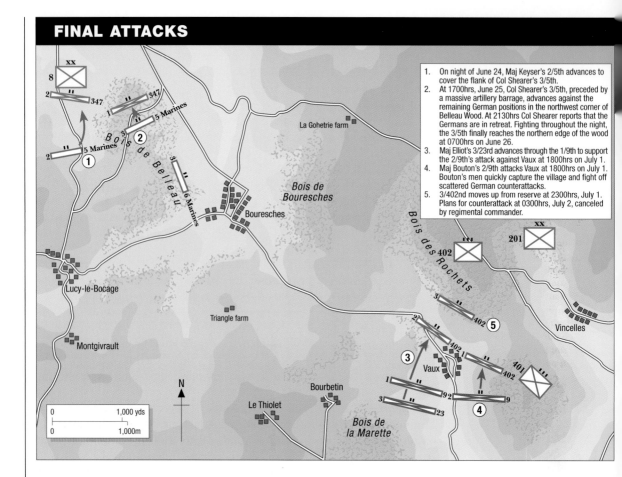

1. On night of June 24, Maj Keyser's 2/5th advances to cover the flank of Col Shearer's 3/5th.
2. At 1700hrs, June 25, Col Shearer's 3/5th, preceded by a massive artillery barrage, advances against the remaining German positions in the northwest corner of Belleau Wood. At 2130hrs Col Shearer reports that the Germans are in retreat. Fighting throughout the night, the 3/5th finally reaches the northern edge of the wood at 0700hrs on June 26.
3. Maj Elliot's 3/23rd advances through the 1/9th to support the 2/9th's attack against Vaux at 1800hrs on July 1.
4. Maj Bouton's 2/9th attacks Vaux at 1800hrs on July 1. Bouton's men quickly capture the village and fight off scattered German counterattacks.
5. 3/402nd moves up from reserve at 2300hrs, July 1. Plans for counterattack at 0300hrs, July 2, canceled by regimental commander.

was too late. With no immediate reserve available the 1/347th tried to reestablish a defensive position along the Lucy–Torcy road. When the companies from the 3rd Reserve Ersatz Regiment arrived they were placed into line. Throughout the night groups of Germans either made their way out of Belleau Wood or surrendered.

At daybreak on June 26, the 16th Company finally reached the northern edge of the wood. Shearer's men had killed or wounded 150 Germans, and captured 300 men and over 30 machine guns. Marine losses totaled over 250. Shearer sent Harbord a simple note: "Belleau Wood now US Marine Corps entirely."

VAUX

While the 4th Brigade was engaged in the desperate struggle for Belleau Wood, the 3rd Brigade supported the Marines, protecting their right flank. When Marine losses became so severe that they were forced to contract their lines, the 3rd Brigade was given responsibility to defend Bouresches. In this period the 23rd and 9th Infantry were under continuous artillery fire. During June 1918 the 3rd Brigade suffered a total of over 300 killed and 1,400 wounded.

As a consequence of the transition of French command from Gen Degoutte to Gen Naulin in mid-June it was decided that plans be developed for a general attack by the 3rd Brigade and French 39th Division to capture the village of Vaux, Hill 204, and the Bois de la Roche.

Using information from displaced residents of Vaux and German prisoners, 2nd Division intelligence officer Col Arthur Conger prepared detailed information about the village. A stonemason who had worked in every house in the village aided in the preparation of plans for attack by providing details for most of the 82 houses in the village. German troop locations were identified and confirmed.

The German 201st Division had responsibility for the sector from Château-Thierry on the east to a point midway between Vaux and Bouresches. The 403rd Infantry Regiment held Château-Thierry, while Hill 204 was defended by the 401st Infantry. The area that included Vaux was the responsibility of the 402nd Infantry Regiment. The 1/402nd defended the area to the east of Vaux, with one company in the village and one on the slope of Hill 204. Two companies were placed in reserve. 2/402nd was assigned the area west of Vaux, with two companies in the Bois de la Roche and two in reserve. The 3/402nd was in reserve several miles to the rear. The regiment totaled 2,100 men on July 1, 1918. The 402nd was assigned six light artillery batteries for support and could call on three heavy position batteries for help.

Orders for the attack were issued to the 3rd Brigade on June 30. The 2/9th under Maj Arthur Bouton was assigned the task of Vaux and the eastern portion of the Bois de la Roche. The regimental machine-gun company and a company of the 2nd Engineers were attached for support.

The 3/23rd under Maj Charles Elliot, with a company from the 2nd Engineers and elements of the brigade machine-gun battalion, were to target Bois de la Roche and a small hill to the west, and to provide support through overhead barrage fire. Trench mortars and 37mm guns would provide fire support. Twelve French batteries, nine 75mm, and three 155mm were to join with American batteries in a 12-hour preparatory barrage. After the initial barrage was complete the artillery would provide a rolling barrage to precede the advance.

Maj Bouton placed two companies in line, one in support, and one in reserve. The lead companies with the engineers were expected to flush out the German defenders. The support company was assigned the

Drawing of Hill 204

Village of Vaux, devastated by American artillery fire.

task of preparing Vaux for an expected German counterattack. Maj Elliot placed three companies in line and one in reserve.

The attack jumped off at 1800hrs on July 1. Advancing close behind the artillery fire the Americans overwhelmed the Germans and by 1900hrs the village was in American hands. Although the Germans had suspected an American attack the intensity of the artillery disrupted their defense of Vaux. At 1500hrs, during the barrage, the 3/402nd was ordered from reserve to move closer to the front. The German survivors of Vaux and supporting units formed a defensive line along the railroad. The Germans organized a counterattack, scheduled to jump off at 0300hrs. The attack would be spearheaded by the 3/402nd, supported by the remnants of the 1st and 2nd battalions.

As the evening wore on, the German regimental commander realized that his men could not recapture Vaux and canceled the attack. News of the canceled attack did not reach the 3/402nd, which advanced as planned, but was shattered as it reached the railroad.

On the right the French 153rd Infantry, 39th Division, attacked the German 401st Infantry and was driven back with heavy losses. On the left, the 1/23rd had not been required to attack in support of Bouton's men. American losses were 46 dead and over 270 wounded and missing. German losses were 250 killed, 160 wounded, and over 500 captured.

With the capture of Vaux, both sides settled into a defensive posture.

German prisoners and Maxim machine guns captured at Vaux.

AFTERMATH

On June 30, French Sixth Army commander Gen Degoutte issued the following order:

In view of the brilliant conduct of the 4th Brigade of the 2nd US Division, which in a spirited fight took Bouresches and the important strongpoint of Belleau Wood, stubbornly defended by a large enemy force, the General of the Sixth Army orders henceforth, in all official papers, the Bois de Belleau shall be named 'Bois de la Brigade de Marine'.

The French Parliament, by unanimous vote, declared that "July 4th, the anniversary of the Declaration of Independence of the United States" would be celebrated as a French national holiday. One company from each regiment in the 2nd Division was withdrawn to create a provisional battalion that was sent to Paris to take part in the parade marking the celebration of American Independence Day. At the same time, the 2nd Division was relieved by the American 26th Division, although elements of the now veteran 2nd Division were kept close to the front due to continued German activity around Château-Thierry.

During the period June 1 to July 10, the 2nd Division had suffered approximately 9,700 casualties. While replacements had been incorporated into the division throughout this period, the division's effective strength on July 10 was still over 2,400 men fewer than it had been on June 1.

American wounded being removed from Vaux after capture by the 3rd Brigade.

The German attack in March, 1918, laid bare the weaknesses of the Allies. By May, the French and British armies had surrendered the initiative to the Germans. The British Army was reeling from the hammer blows of Operation *Michael* and British staff had begun planning for the possibility of evacuation to England. The French had witnessed the sundering of their lines along the Chemin des Dames, opening the road to Paris. Circumstances required that the largely untested American Army be thrust into a battle no one had planned for.

In the course of late May and June, the Americans learned very hard lessons about the reality of warfare. The inadequacies of their training and shortcomings of their officers were measured in the length of the casualty lists. The real impact of the American battles of June 1918 was not in the ground taken or villages captured. Although the immediate result of the battle of Belleau Wood was to stop the German advance towards Paris and allow the French Army to reorganize, there was much more at stake. When the 2nd Division confronted the Germans at Belleau Wood, the Americans and Germans entered into a final struggle for moral ascendancy over the battlefield and the final outcome of the war. Moral ascendancy on the battlefield meant controlling the rhythm of engagements, dictating the outcome of battles, and boosting the morale of the troops. Conversely, possession of moral ascendancy demoralized your enemies and eroded their will to resist. The rapid string of Allied victories following the collapse of the German offensive in July 1918 bears testimony to the impact of the battle of Belleau Wood.

In the aftermath of Belleau Wood the Germans came to recognize that fundamental changes on the battlefield had begun. A German veteran wrote:

The American … had nerve; we must give him credit for that; but he also displayed a savage roughness. 'The Americans kill everybody' was the cry of terror…which for a long time stuck in the bones of our men.

THE BATTLEFIELD TODAY

The Aisne/Marne Cemetery and Memorial is located outside the village of Belleau, just north of Belleau Wood. The 42-acre park includes a memorial chapel and visitor's building. The cemetery and memorial were constructed by the American Battle Monuments Commission and dedicated on May 30, 1937.

The cemetery is laid out as a "T." A long avenue leads from the visitor center towards the chapel. The chapel is built on the rising hillside while 2,288 gravesites extend to both sides, curving slightly around each side of the chapel. The chapel includes three columns on which are engraved scenes of soldiers preparing for a bayonet charge, automatic riflemen, artillery observers, and machine-gun crews. Over the entrance is a figure of a crusader in armor, flanked by shields of the United States and France. Above the entrance is written, "The Names Recorded on These Walls Are Those of American Soldiers Who Fought in This Region and Who Sleep in Unknown Graves." Within the chapel are small alcoves in which are listed the names of 1,060 missing in action.

An altar dominates the main section of the chapel. Across the front of the altar is inscribed "Peaceful They Rest in Glory Everlasting." A stained-glass window rises directly behind the altar depicting St Michael triumphing over evil. On the left of the altar another window depicts the crusader St Louis, while on the right a window includes the patron saint of France, St Denis.

Adjoining the cemetery is Belleau Wood. The 200-acre wood is maintained by the American Battle Monuments Commission. Within the wood remains of shell holes and trenches are still visible. Various weapons found in and around the wood, including artillery and mortars, are displayed as part of several monuments to the Marines. In the northwest corner of the wood are the remains of the hunting lodge that served as a German battalion headquaters until overrun by the 43rd Company. There is a nearby German cemetery where 8,625 men are buried.

Commander of the 4th Brigade, Brig Gen James G. Harbord, spoke at the dedication of the Aisne/Marne Cemetery and predicted:

Now and then, a veteran ... will come here to live again the brave days of that distant June. Here will be raised the altars of patriotism; here will be renewed the vows of sacrifice and consecration to country. Hither will come our countrymen in hours of depression, and even of failure, and take new courage from this shrine of great deeds.

BIBLIOGRAPHY

Allen, Hervey, *Toward the Flame*, George H. Doran Company, New York, 1926
Asprey, Robert, *The German High Command at War*, Morrow, New York, 1991
Asprey, Robert, *At Belleau Wood*, University of North Texas Press, Denton, 1996
Boyd, Thomas, *Through the Wheat*, University of Nebraska Press, Lincoln, 2000
Brannen, Carl Andrew, *Over There*, Texas A & M Press, College Station, 1996
Broun, Heywood, *Our Army at the Front*, Charles Scribner's Sons, Woodbridge, 1922
Brown, Ronald J., *A Few Good Men*, Presidio, New York, 2001
Clark, George, *Devil Dogs*, Presidio, New York, 2000
Coffin, Edward, *The War to End All Wars*, Wisconsin Press, Madison, 1986
Cron, Hermann, *Imperial German Army 1914–1918*, Helion & Company, Solihull, 2002
Farwell, Byron, *Over There*, Norton, New York, 1999
German Army Handbook, April 1918, Hippocrene Books, New York, 1977
Gibbons, Floyd, *And They Thought We Wouldn't Fight*, George H. Doran Company, New York, 1918
Gudmundsson, Bruce I., *Stormtroop Tactics*, Praeger, Westport, 1989
Hamilton, Craig and Louise Corbin, (Ed.) *Echoes From Over There*, Soldiers Publishing Company, 1919
Harries, Meirion and Susie Harries, *The Last Days of Innocence, America at War, 1917–1918*, Random House, New York, 1997
Heller, Charles and William Stofft, *America's First Battles, 1776–1965*, Kansas Press, Lawrence, 1986
Henry, Mark R., *US Marine Corps in World War I 1917–1918*, Osprey Publishing, Oxford, 1999
Jamieson, Perry D., *Crossing the Deadly Ground*, University of Alabama Press, Tuscaloosa, 1994
Kean, Robert Winthrop, *Dear Marraine 1917–1919*, 1969
Liggett, Hunter, *AEF, Ten Years Ago in France*, Scholar's Bookshelf, Cranbury, 2005
Mackin, Elton E., *Suddenly We Didn't Want to Die*, Presidio, New York, 1993
Marshall, George C., *Memoirs of My Services in the War 1917–1918*, Houghton Mifflin, Boston, 1976
McClellan, Edwin N., *The United States Marine Corps in the First World War*, University Press of the Pacific, Honolulu, 2002
Moiser, John, *The Myth of the Great War*, Harper Collins, New York, 2001
Palmer, Frederick, *America in France*, Greenwood Press, Westport, 1975
Rice, Earle Jr, *Battle of Belleau Wood*, Lucent Books, Chicago, 1996
Scanlon, William T., *God Have Mercy on Us*, Houghton Mifflin Company, Boston, 1929
Sellers, James McBrayer, *World War I Memoirs*, Brass Hat Press, 1997
Suskind, Richard, *Do You Want To Live Forever*, Bantam, New York, 1964
Suskind, Richard, *The Battle of Belleau Wood*, Macmillan, New York, 1969
Spaulding, Oliver and John Wright, *The Second Division American Expeditionary Force In France, 1917–1919*, Battery Press, Nashville, 1989
Terraine, John, *To Win a War, 1918 The Year of Victory*, Cassell, London, 1978
Toland, John, *No Man's Land*, Smithmark, New York, 1980
Westover, Wendell, *Suicide Battalions*, Putnam, New York, 1929
Wise, Frederic, *A Marine Tells It To You*, MCA Heritage, 1981

INDEX

Figures in **bold** refer to illustrations

Adams, Lt Col John 85, 86
aircraft **33**, **47**
artillery
    at Belleau Wood 47–48, 49, **50**, 87
    at Cantigny 32, **36–38**
    French 21, 32, 47–48, 49, 89
    German 14, 20, 51–52, **56**
    US **6**, 18, **31**, **50**
    at Vaux 89

barbed wire **7**, **36–38**
Bathelemont 26–27
Belleau Wood **10**, 23, 42–54, 59–88, **73**, **80–82**
Berry, Maj Benjamin 49, 51, 53, 58–63, 63, 65–67, 70, 73
Bischoff, Maj 59–60, 72, 75
Bissell, Lt John 41, 42
Bois de la Roche 89
Bois Gros Jean 87
Bouresches
    Allied capture 60, 61, 63–66, **65–66**
    Allied defense 67, 70, 71, 75, 83, 84, 87
    part in Allied plans 23
Bouton, Maj Arthur 89–90
British Army
    attitude to US Army 9–10
    defensive measures 8, 10
    tactical doctrine 16
Brown, Col Preston **28**, 42–43, 45–46, 53
Bruchmuller, Georg 14
Bullard, Gen Robert **26**, 27, 32, 35, 39
Bundy, Gen Omar **28**
    and Belleau Wood 45–46, 53–54, 59, 67, 75, 78, 84–87
    Pershing's doubts about 27
    plans 23

Cantigny 20, 22–23, 30–39, **30–31**, **33**, **36–39**
Carre, Capt Alphonse de 75
Case, Capt Phillip 66, 85
Cates, Lt Clifton 64
Catlin, Albertus 13, 46–48, 50–51, 60–61, 63
cemeteries **92**, 93
Champillon 47, 54
Château-Thierry 20, 23, 41–42, **42–45**
Chemin des Dames offensive: map **72**

Cole, Maj Edward 46, 65–66, 73
Conachy, Capt Peter 58, 60, 67
Conger, Col Arthur 89
Conner, Col Fox 40
Conta, Gen von 49, 50, 72
Cooke, Lt Elliot 67, 74, 78, 79, 82
Crowther, Capt 54, 55, 56

Dederer, Capt 70
Degoutte, Gen
    and Belleau Wood 45–46, 48–49, 52–53, 59
    plans 23, 42–43
    promotion 84
    verdict on Marine performance 91
Duchene, Gen 40
Dunbeck, Capt Charles 74, 78
Duncan, Capt Donald 61, 64

Elliot, Maj Charles 61, 64, 89–90
Ely, Col Hansen 31, 34, 35, **35**, 39
entrenching equipment **36–38**

Feland, Logan 13, 54, 57, 65–66, 79, 84, 85
Feldpausch, Private **34**
field kitchens **55**
Foch, Gen Ferdinand **13**
    and *Blücher* 23, 39, 40
    role 9
    and US deployment 12–13, 22
French Army **9**
    artillery 21, 32, 47–48, 49, 89
    attitude to US Army 9–10
    and Belleau Wood 45–49, 51, 52–53, 58, 59, 61, 66, 67
    and *Blücher* 22–23, 39–40, 42–45
    condition in late 1917 7
    defensive measures 8, 10
    and Montdidier–Noyon sector 71
    mutiny 24
    overview 20–21
    tactical doctrine 16
    and US training 16–17, **16**
    and Vaux 89–90
French Army: sub-units
    10th Colonial Division 41, 66, 67
    10th Colonial Regiment 61
    39th Division 51
    167th Division 52–53, 58, 59
    Chasseurs 49

Garrett, Maj Franklin 84
Geer, Corp 56
German Army
    commanders 14

Hindenburg's Traveling Circus 29–30
marching **8**
order of battle 21
organization 19
overview 19–20
plans 8, 22
storm troopers **7**, 8, 20, 29, 30
tactics 14, 19, 20
training 19
uniforms **39**
weapons 19–20
German Army: divisions
    5th Prussian Guards 49, 58, 67, 73, 74
    10th 20, 42, 49, 60, 67, 72, 74
    25th 35, 39
    28th 20, 54, 67, 71, 72, 74, 75
    36th 20, 49
    82nd 28, 32, 35, 39
    87th 20, 85
    197th 49–50, 54, 58, 67, 72, 74
    201st 89
    231st 40, 41–42, 49
    237th 20, 42, 49, 54, 59–60, 85
German Army: regiments
    3rd Reserve Ersatz 87–88
    7th Bavarian Landwehr 26
    7th Saxon Jägers 56
    26th Saxon Jägers 52
    40th Fusiliers 72, 74–75, 83
    83rd 35, 39
    109th Grenadiers 83
    110th 75
    259th 30
    270th 29, 32, 35
    271st 29, 32, 34, 35
    272nd 28, 29, 32, 34, 35
    273rd 54, 58
    347th 85, 87–88
    398th 60
    401st 89, 90
    402nd 89, 90
    403rd 89
    460th 54
    461st 52, 59–60, 62, 72, 75, **80–82**, 85
Gibbons, Floyd 58–59, 63
Goureaucourt 26

Haig, Gen Douglas 10, 40
Hamilton, Capt George 54, 55–56, 57, 58
Harbord, Brig Gen James **12**
    and Belleau Wood 43, 46–48, 51–2, 58–61, 63, 65–67, 70, 73, 75, 78–79, 83–88

overview 13
plans 23
speech at Aisne/Marne Cemetery 93
Hartlieb, Maj von 72, 75, 85
Hill 126 49
Hill 133 60
Hill 142 46, 48, 49, 53–59, 65, 79–83, 87
Hill 165 47
Hill 169 86
Hill 204 45, 54, 67, 89, **89**
Hoffman, Gunnery Sgt Charles 56–57
Holcomb, Maj Thomas 48, 60, 61, 65, 83, 84, 87
Houghton, Capt Charles H. 41
Hubbard, Capt Samuel 40
Hughes, Maj John 70–74, 78–79, 84, 87
Hutier, Oskar von 14, 20, 35–39, 71

insignia **80–82**
intelligence 52–53, 57, 59, 65–66, 89

Keyser, Maj Ralph 84, 87

Lee, Lt Col 63, 65, 70, 73, 84
Lewis, Brig Gen Edward 27, 61
Lloyd George, David 9, 24
Lucy-le-Bocage 46, 47, **55**, 71, 87
Ludendorff, Gen Eric
 attempts to demoralize US troops 25
 and *Blücher* 50, 71
 overview 14
 plans 8, 10, 22, 39

Maizey raid 28–29
Malone, Col Paul 46, 47, 48, 64
Les Mares Farm 20, 47, 49–50, 52, 54
Marshall, Lt Col George 31, 32
Matthews, Lt 75, 78
medical treatment **83**
Messersmith, Maj Robert 65
Milner, Lt Drinkard 78, 79
Montdidier–Noyon sector 45, 67, 71

Nauline, Gen 84–85
Neville, Col Wendell 46–47, 51, 54, 57–58, 75, 79, 84

Operation
 Blücher 10, 22–23, 39–40
 Georgette 10, 14, 22, 26, 39
 Gneisenau 22
 Michael 8, 22, 39
orders of battle 21
Otto, LtCol Ernst 62

Paris: German threat to 22, 23, 40, 45
Paris–Metz road 45, 54
Paris Farm 70
Pershing, Gen John J. **13**, **26**
 and Belleau Wood 52
 and doctrine 15–16

establishment of Army in France 24–25
and integration of US troops 9–10, 12–13
and Marshall 32
and US commanders 27
Pétain, Henri 7, 24, 25, 45
poison gas 27, 65, 66, 83, 84
Portuguese forces 10
Premont 47
Pyramid Farm 48, 51

Ragueneau, Gen 40
recruitment posters **17–18**
religious services **70**
Roosevelt, Lt Archie 26–27
Roosevelt, Maj Theodore 26

St Martin Wood 46, 48, 83, 85
Schoonover, Frank: illustrations by **29**, **33**, **65**
Seicheprey raid (1918) 29–30, **31**
Shearer, Maj Maurice 47–49, 70, 75, 83–84, 86–88
Sibley, Maj Berton 51, 53, 60–61, 63, 65–67, 70, 87
signal teams **74**

tactics
 German 14, 19, 20
 US 16–17, 61, 79
tanks **23**, **28**, **33**
traffic jams **46**
training 16–17, **16**, 19, 25
trenches **27**
Turrill, Maj James 47, 53–55, 57–58, 60, 65, 79–85

uniforms **12**, **25**, **39**, **80–82**
Upton, Col LeRoy 48, 64
US Army
 arrival in France 24–26
 commanders 12–14
 defensive positions **62**
 German attempts to demoralize 25, 31
 German propaganda against 7
 integration into Allied forces 9–10, 12–13, 24, 26
 multi-ethnicity 17, **17**
 order of battle 21
 organization 15, 17–18
 overview 15–19
 plans 22–23
 tactics 16–17, 61, 79
 training 16, **16**, 25
 weapons 18, 19
US Army: brigades
 3rd Brigade 28–29, 45–48, 51, 53, 61–65, 67, 70, 84, 87–90
 4th Brigade 12, 24, 27, 43, 45–87
US Army: divisions
 1st **26**
  arrival in France 24, 25
  at Cantigny 22–23, 30–39, **30–31**, **33**, **36–39**
  composition 19
  early ops 26–27

2nd
 at Belleau Wood 42–87
 casualties 91
 at Champillon 23
 composition 19, 24
 early ops 27–29
 training 25
3rd 23, 24, 26, 40–42, **45**, 51, 85
26th 24, 25, 26, 27, 29–30, **31**, 32
42nd 24, 26, 27
US Army: regiments
 2nd Engineers 57, 70, 79
 7th 85–87
 9th 28–29, 46, 48, 51, 61, 64–65, 67, 70, 84, 88, 89–90
 11th Engineers 26
 12th 49
 15th 49
 16th 32, 39
 17th 49
 18th 27, **27**, 32, 34, 35
 23rd 28, 46, 47, 51, 53, 61, 70, 84, 87, 88, 89–90
 26th 49, 51
 28th **28**, 31–39, **36–38**
 30th 35, 51
 102nd 30
 104th 29–30
US Marine Corps
 5th Marine Regiment 24, **25**, 46–87, **80–82**
 6th Marine Regiment 24, 46–79, 84, 87
 expansion 17
 recruitment posters **18**
 replacements 18
 snipers **6**
 training **16**, 17
 uniforms **12**, **25**, **80–82**

Vaux 45, 60, 88–90, **90–91**
Veuilly and Veuilly Wood 47, 49
La Voie du Châtel 46, 50, 57

Waddill, Maj 61, 64
Wass, Capt Lester 74, 78, 79
weapons
 bayonets **15**, 19
 German infantry 19–20
 grenades **16**, 20, **80–82**
 Karabiner 98 19–20
 machine guns
  French **9**
  German 20, **36–38**, **86**, **90**
  US 19, **36–38**, **52**, **59**, **73**, **80–82**
 rifles 19
 US infantry 19
 US organization 18
Williams, Capt Lloyd 49, 58, 66, 74
Wilson, Woodrow 12, 24
Winans, Capt Russell 83–84, 85
Wise, Lt Col Frederic **48**
 at Belleau Wood 47–50, 58, 61, 66–67, 73–79, 83–85, 87
 on training 16
 overview 13–14

Zane, Capt Randolf 63–64